Your World In Color is a picture book that I created following the monochromatic picture book "Seeing Past Color." I didn't originally have any intention of doing a follow up book, but after further reflection I felt a deep need to share the light that came from within the black and white photo's. This light is representative of the need to nurture and care for animals, the environment, nature & all types of life, even in it's smallest forms. I hope that this book will encourage children to put down their electronic devices for a moment and take the time to cherish life & beauty in it's many forms. If or when they do decide to go back to their technology, my hope is the kids will be inspired to use those platforms to minimize their footprints on earth & improve the lives of their selves and others. This book serves as a personal reminder to me to be grateful for all the Lord has blessed me with and that I would not want to live in a world without color.

You are welcome to write your own stories or draw your own pictures in the blank spaces around the photographs.

Thanks To God & My Family I Love U All
In Loving Memory Of Those We've Lost

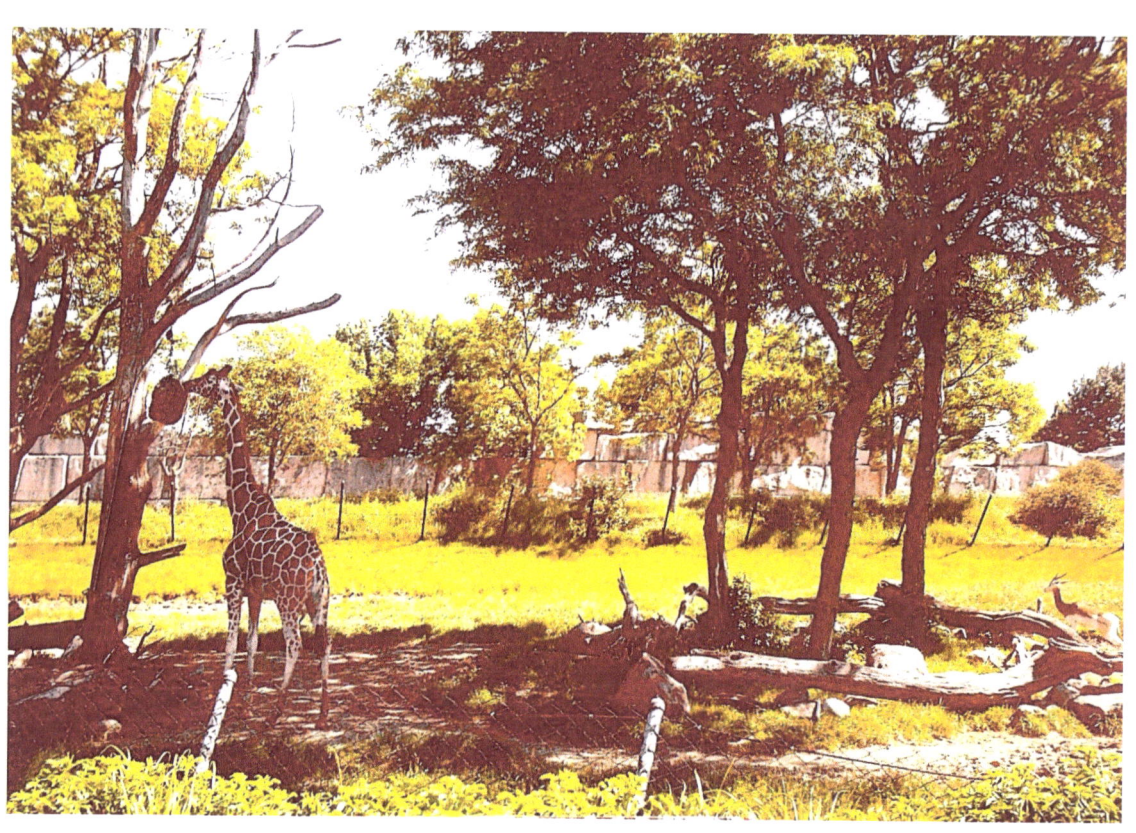

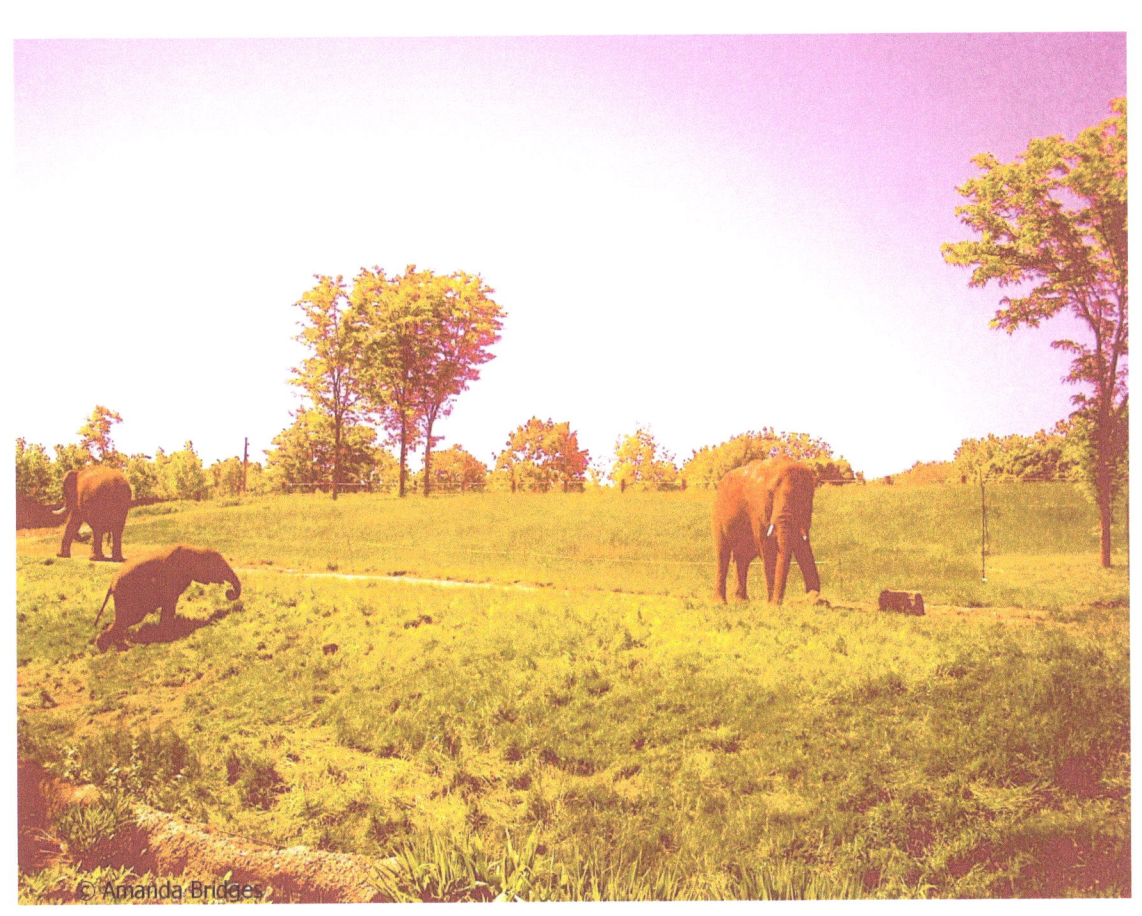

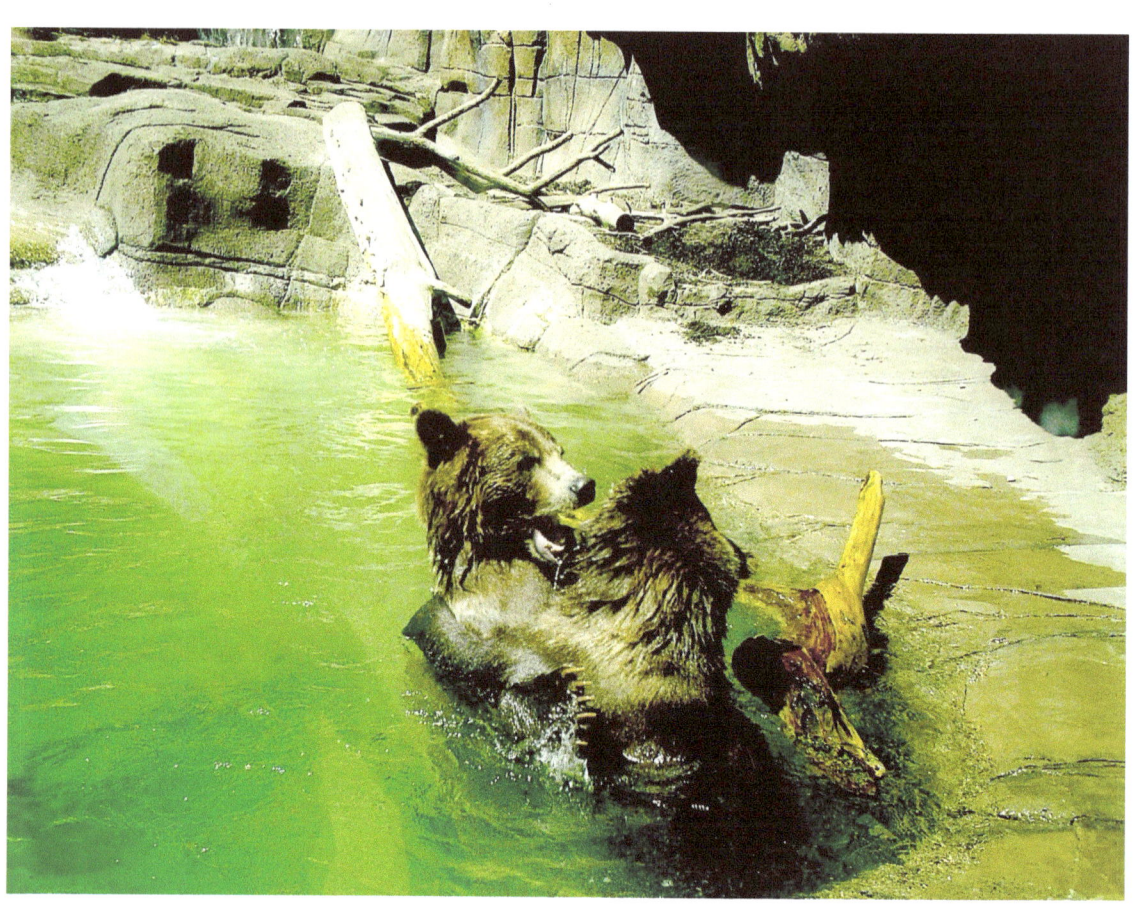

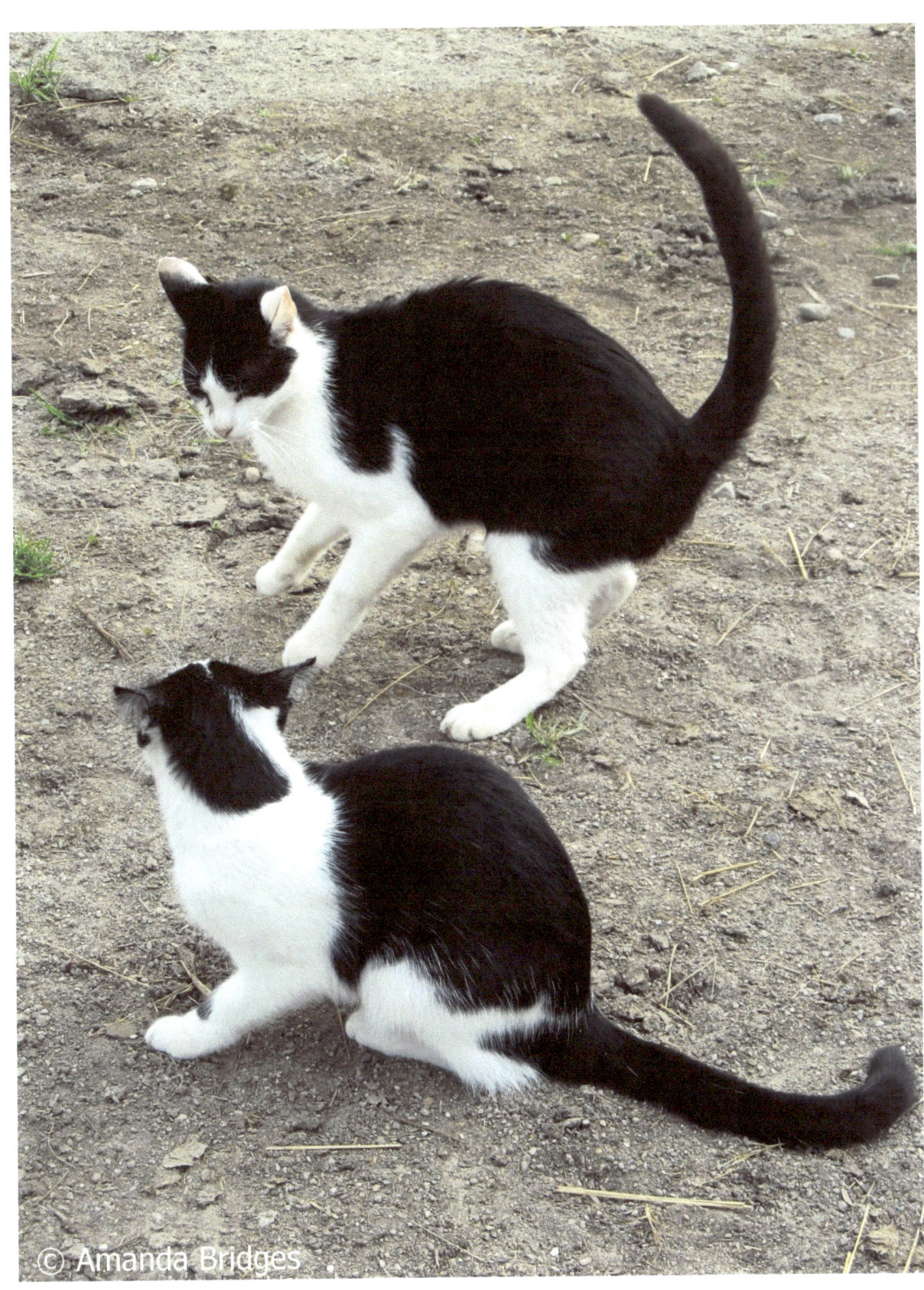

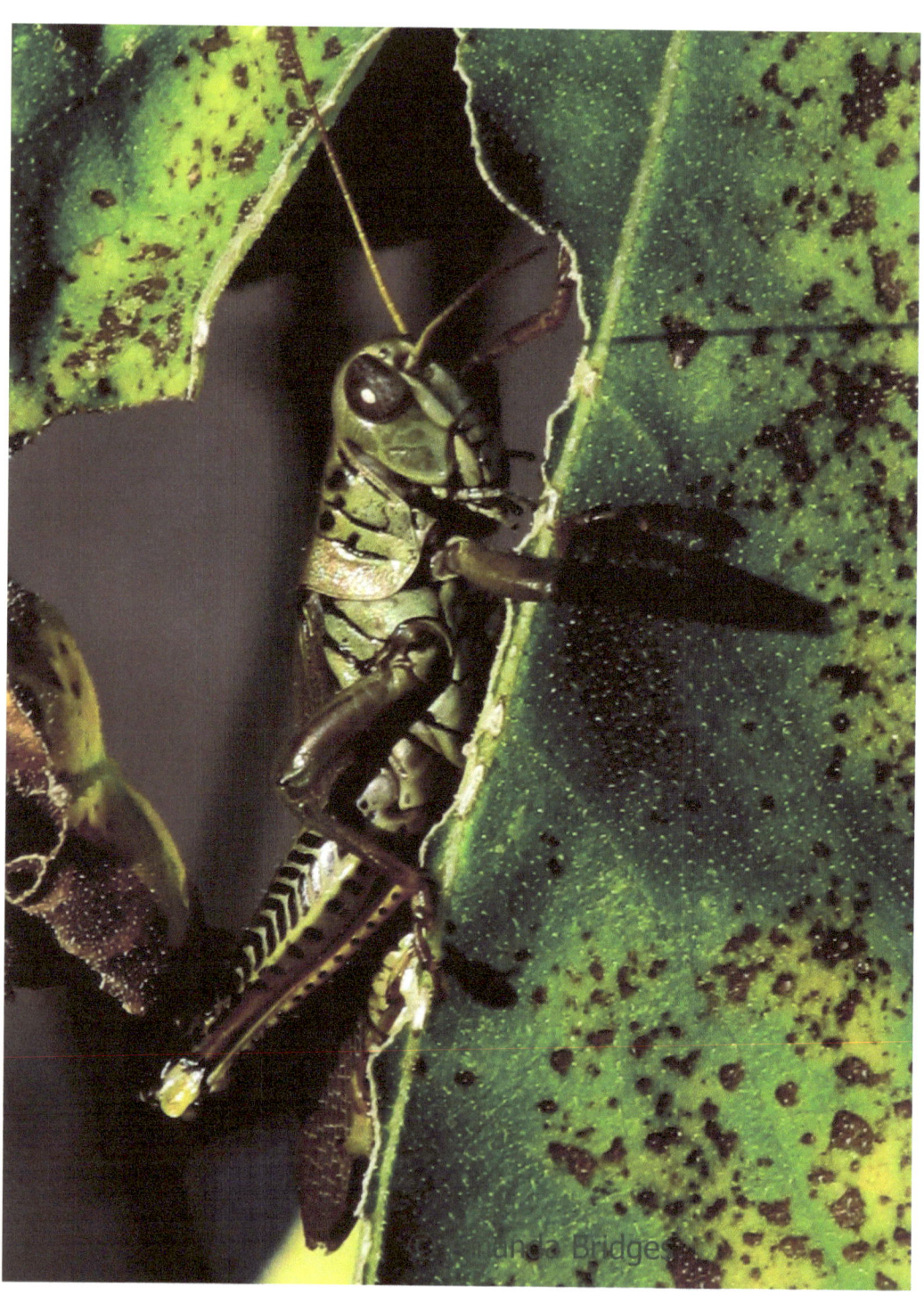

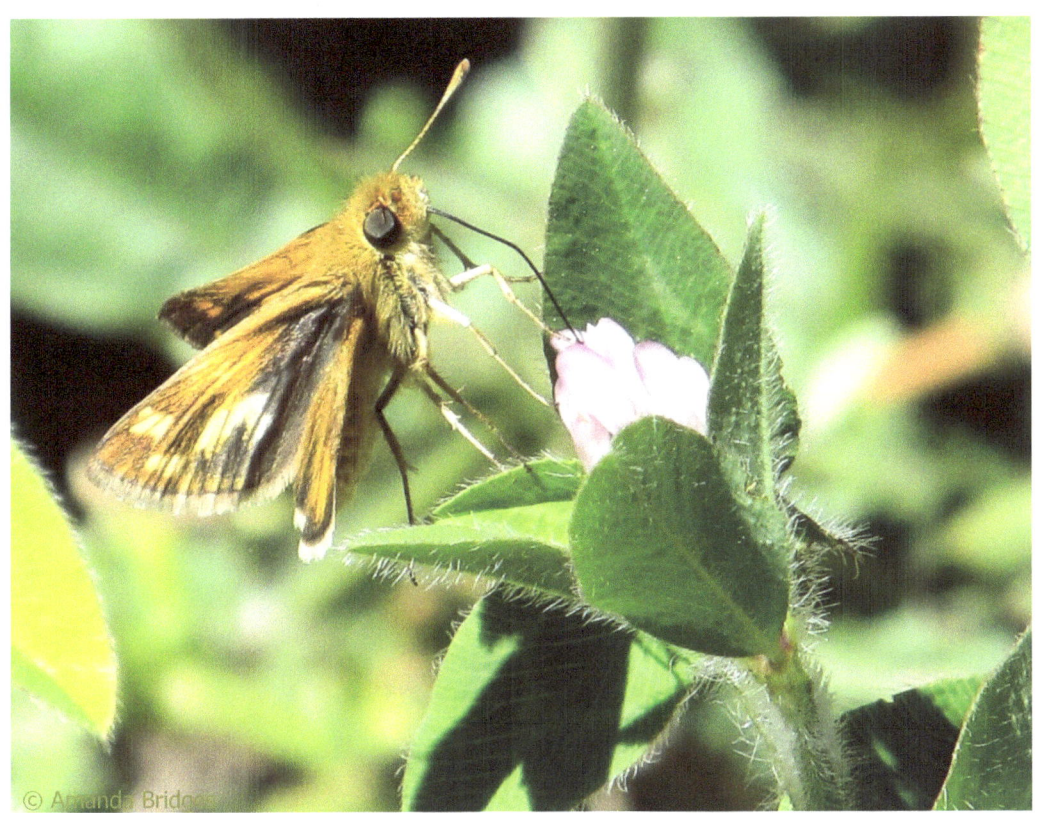

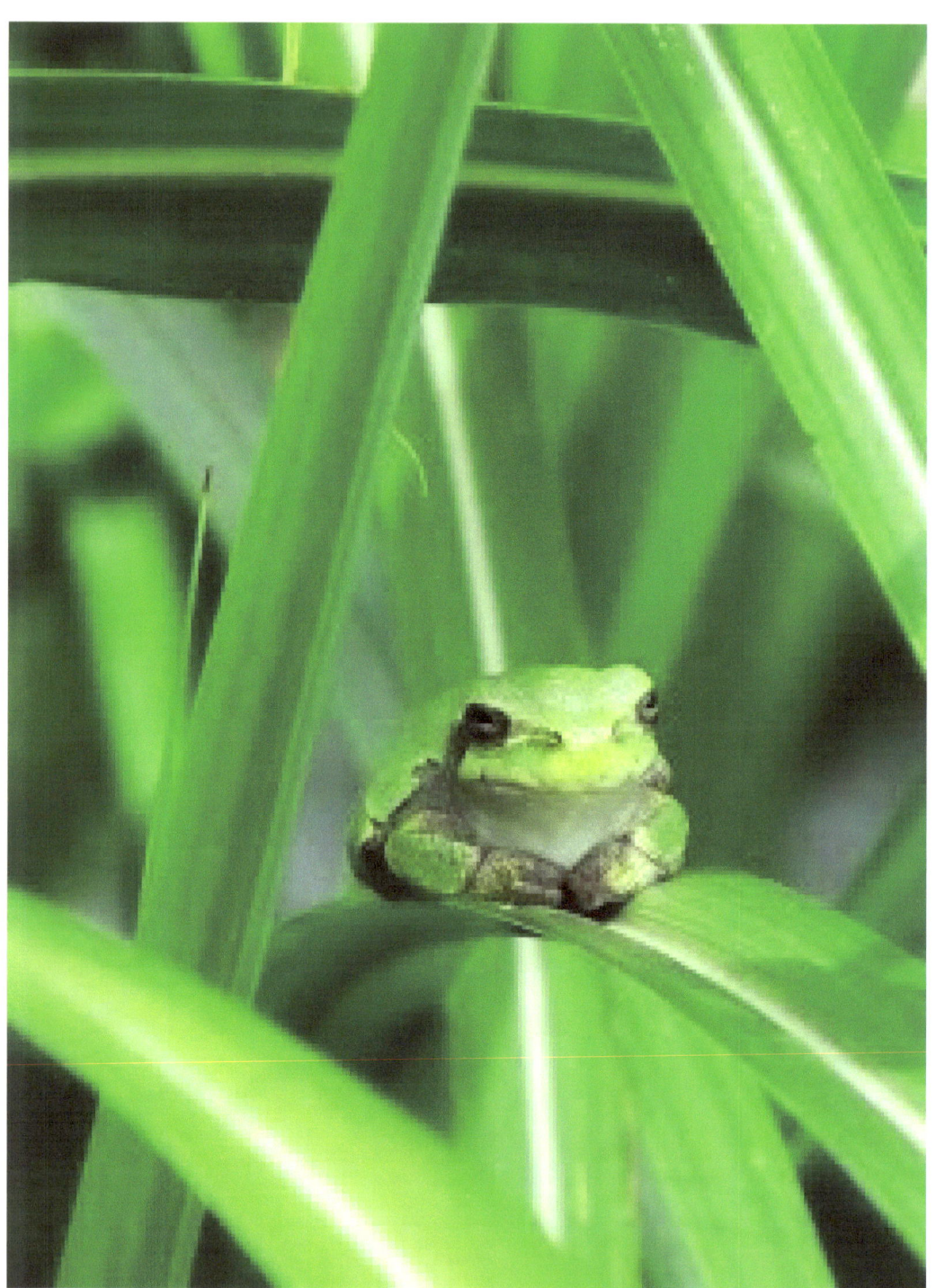

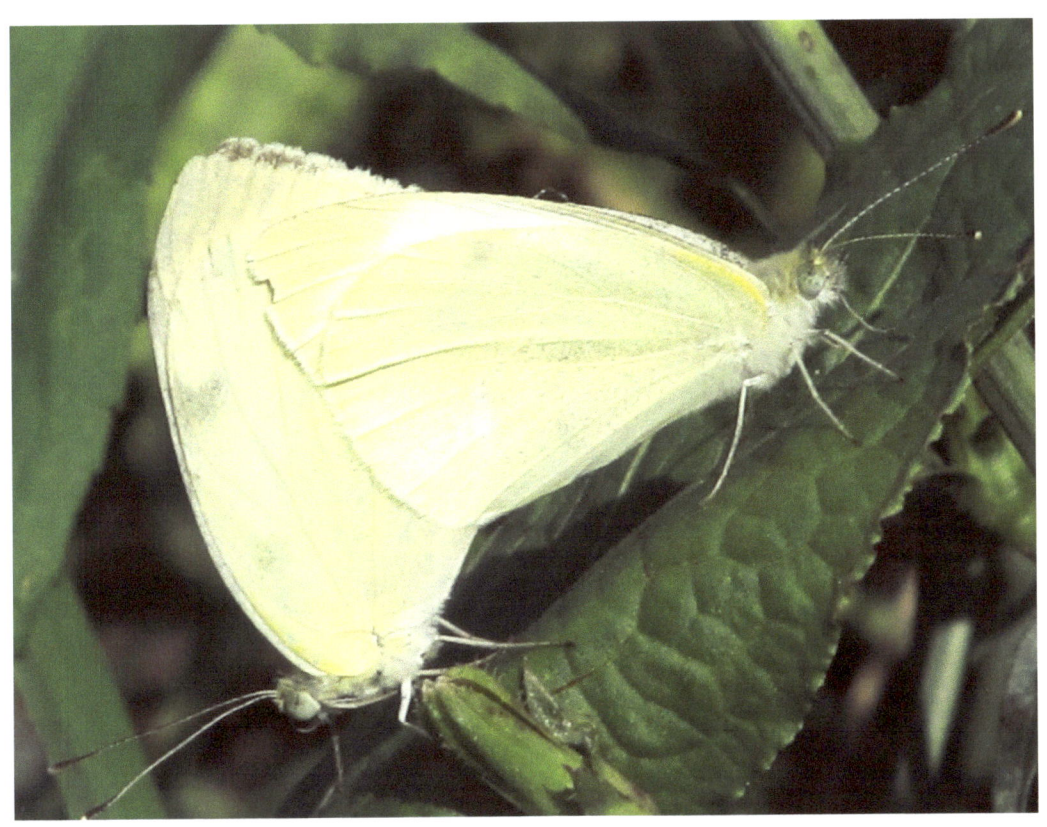

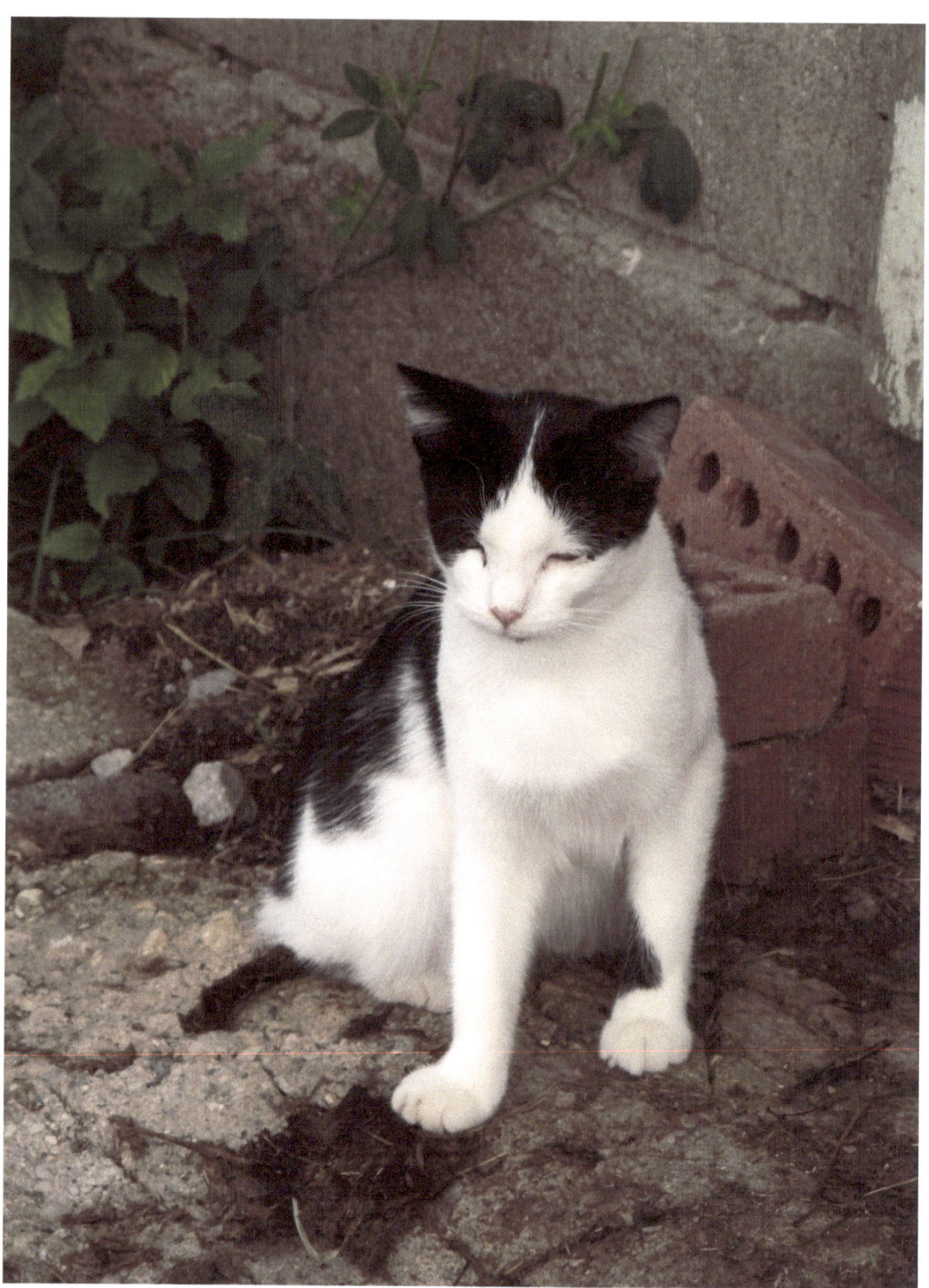

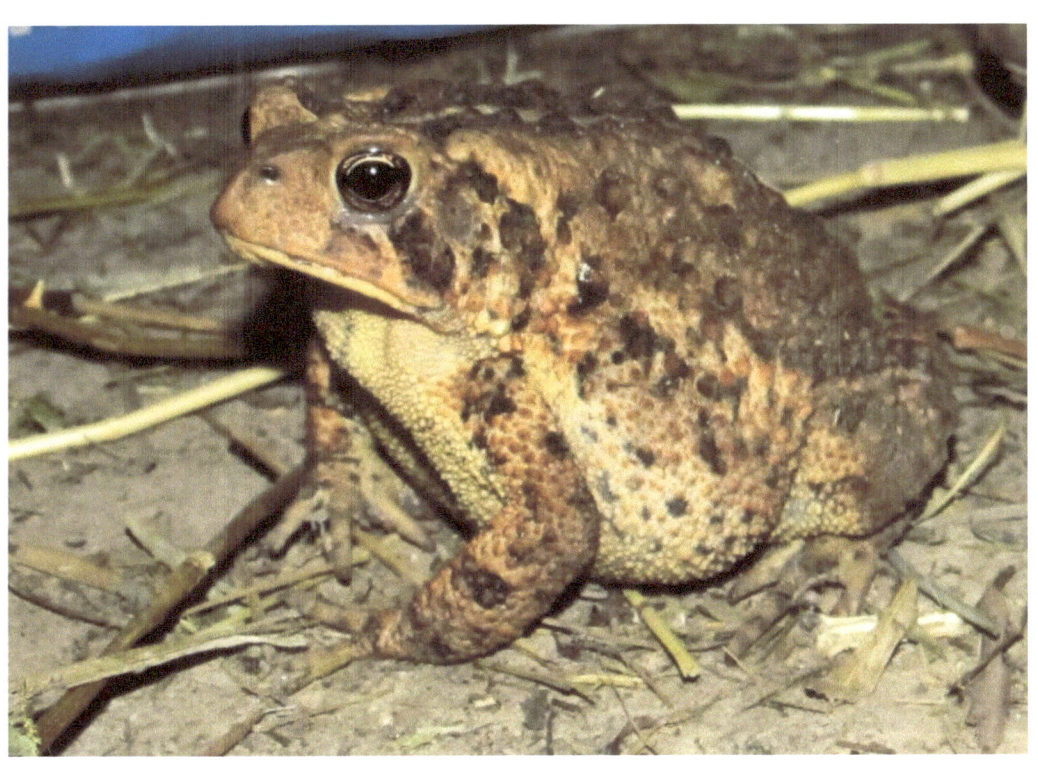

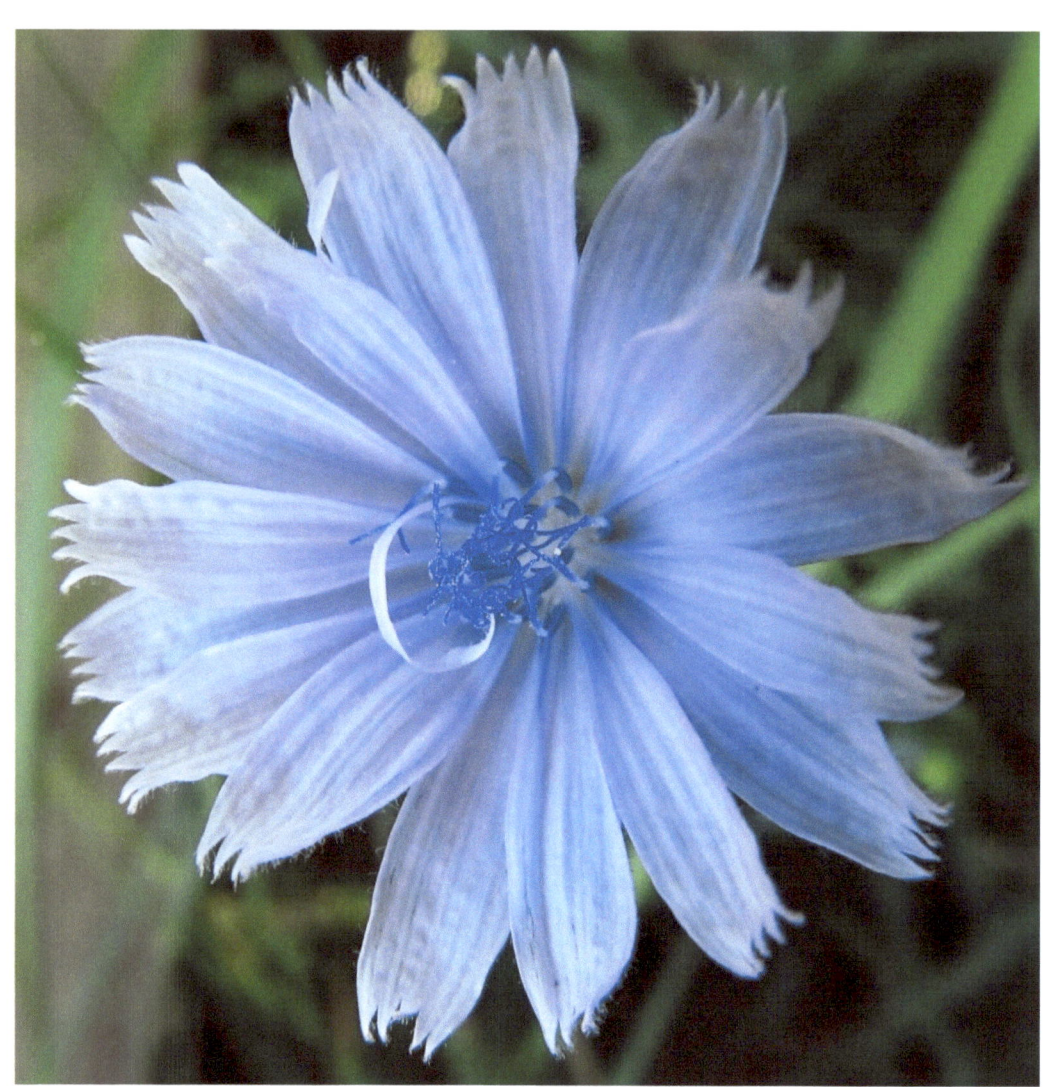

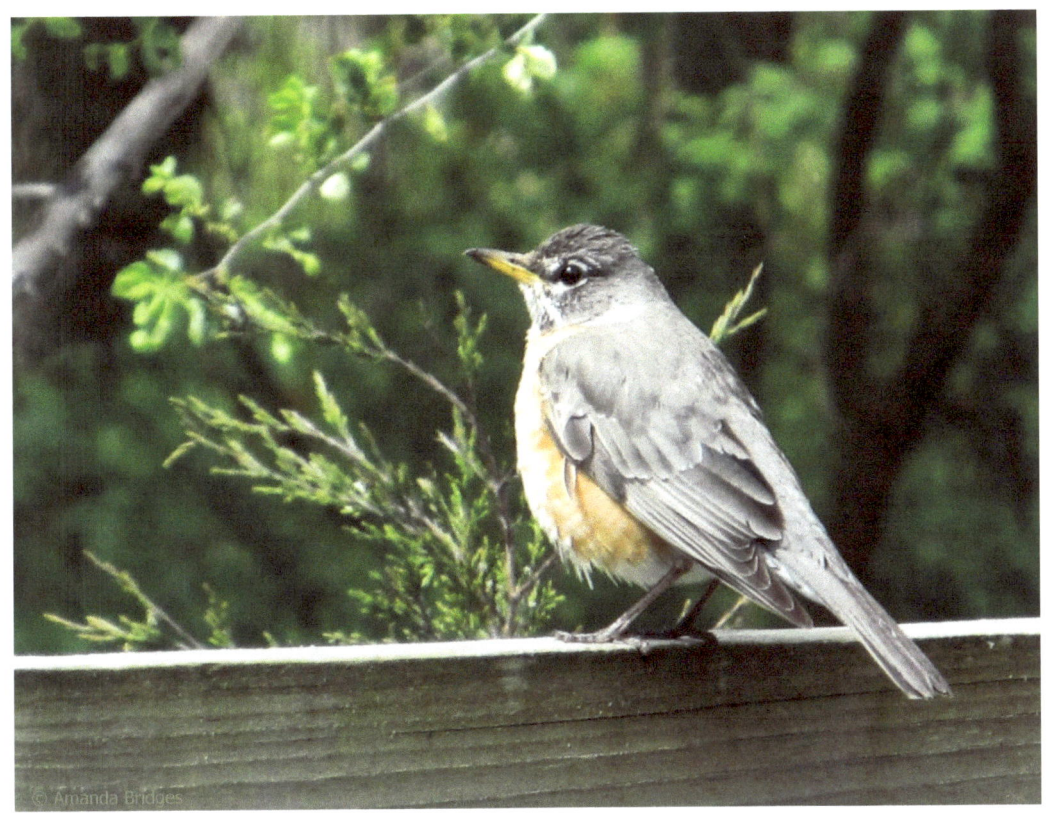

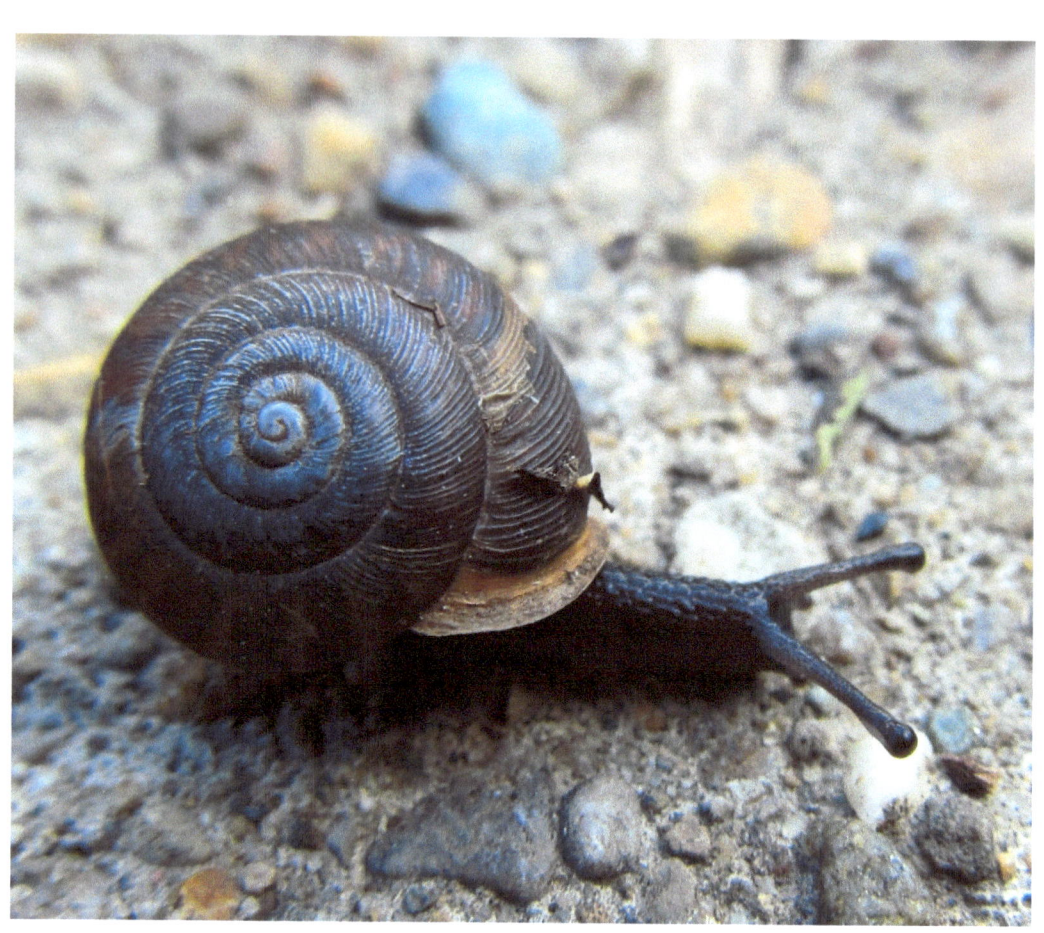

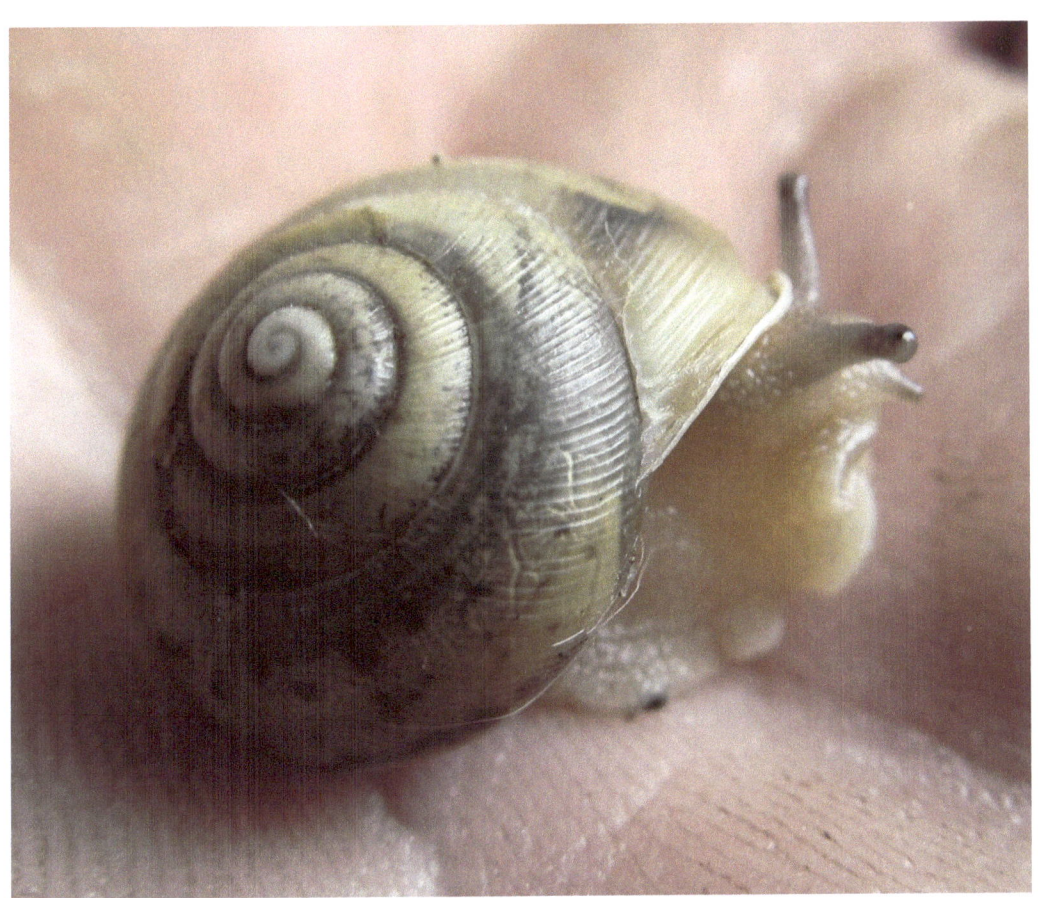

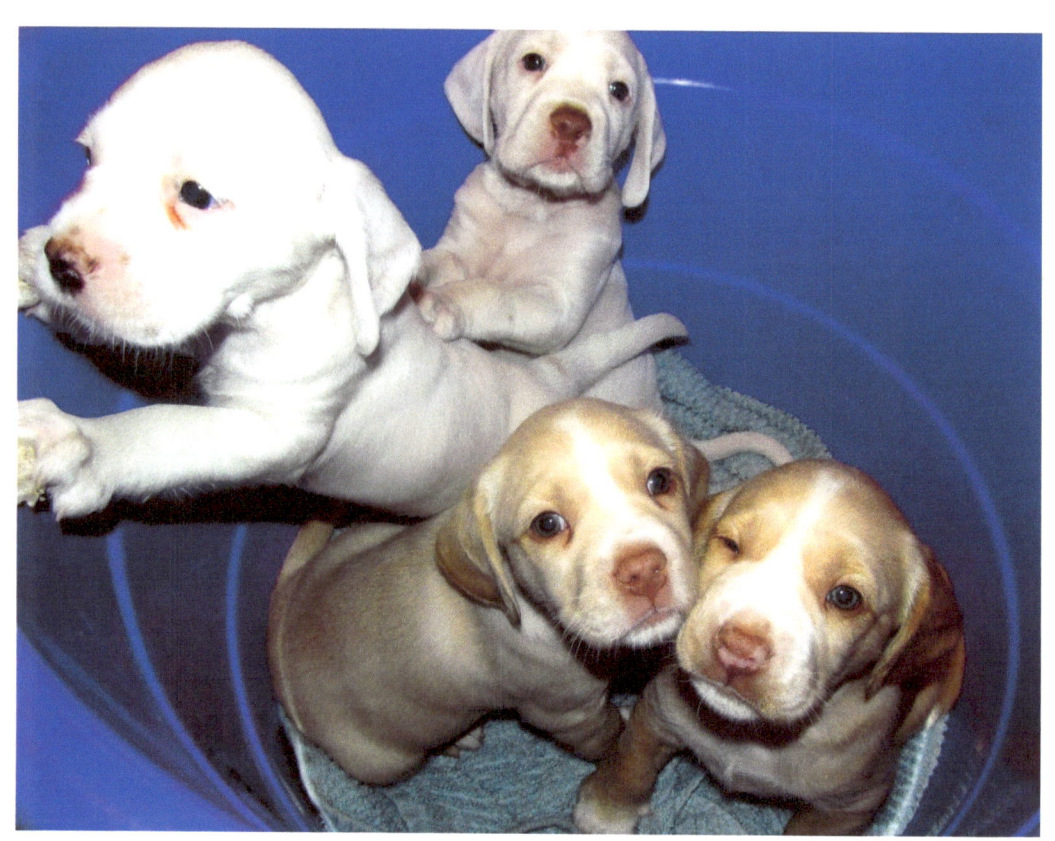

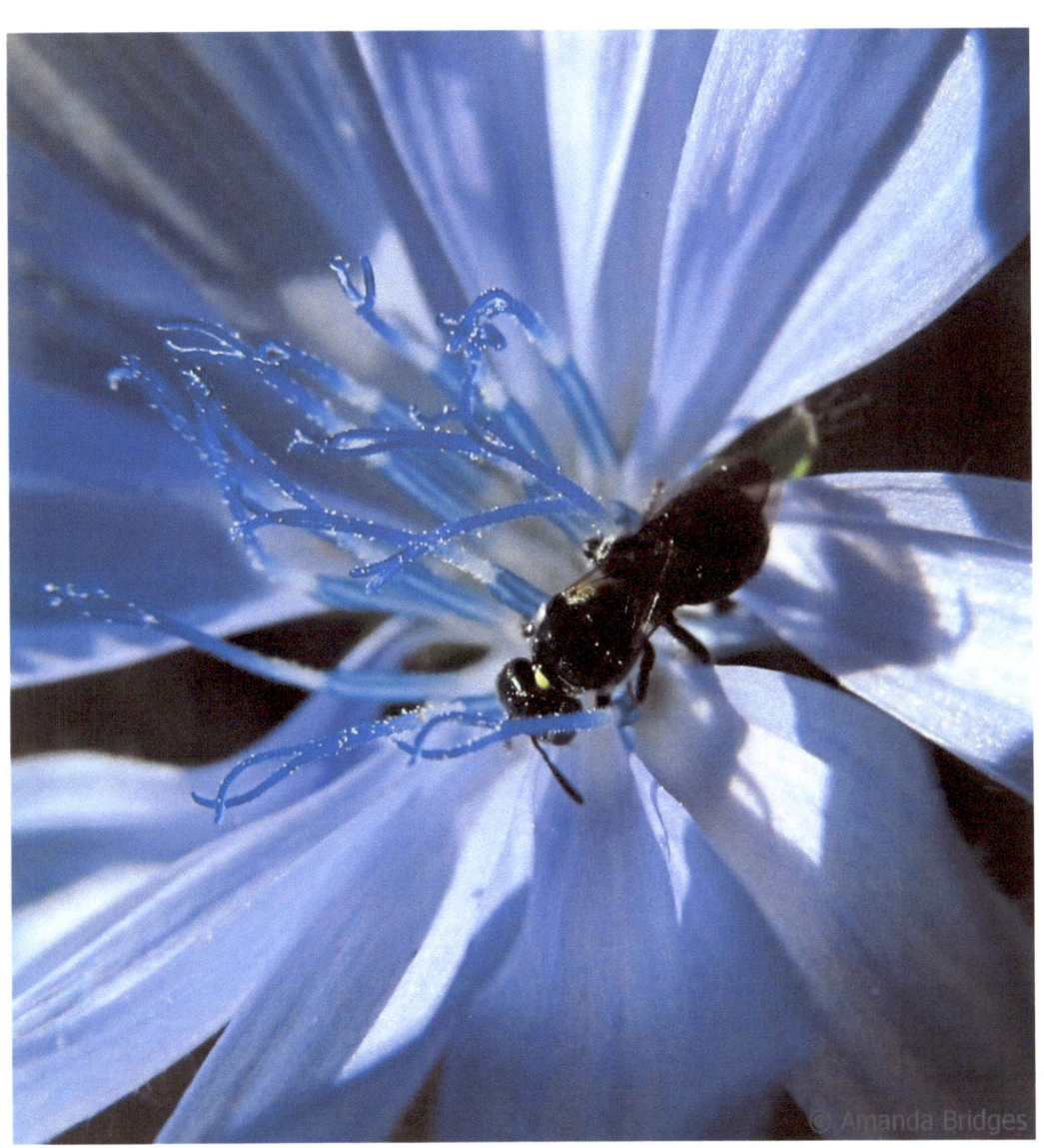

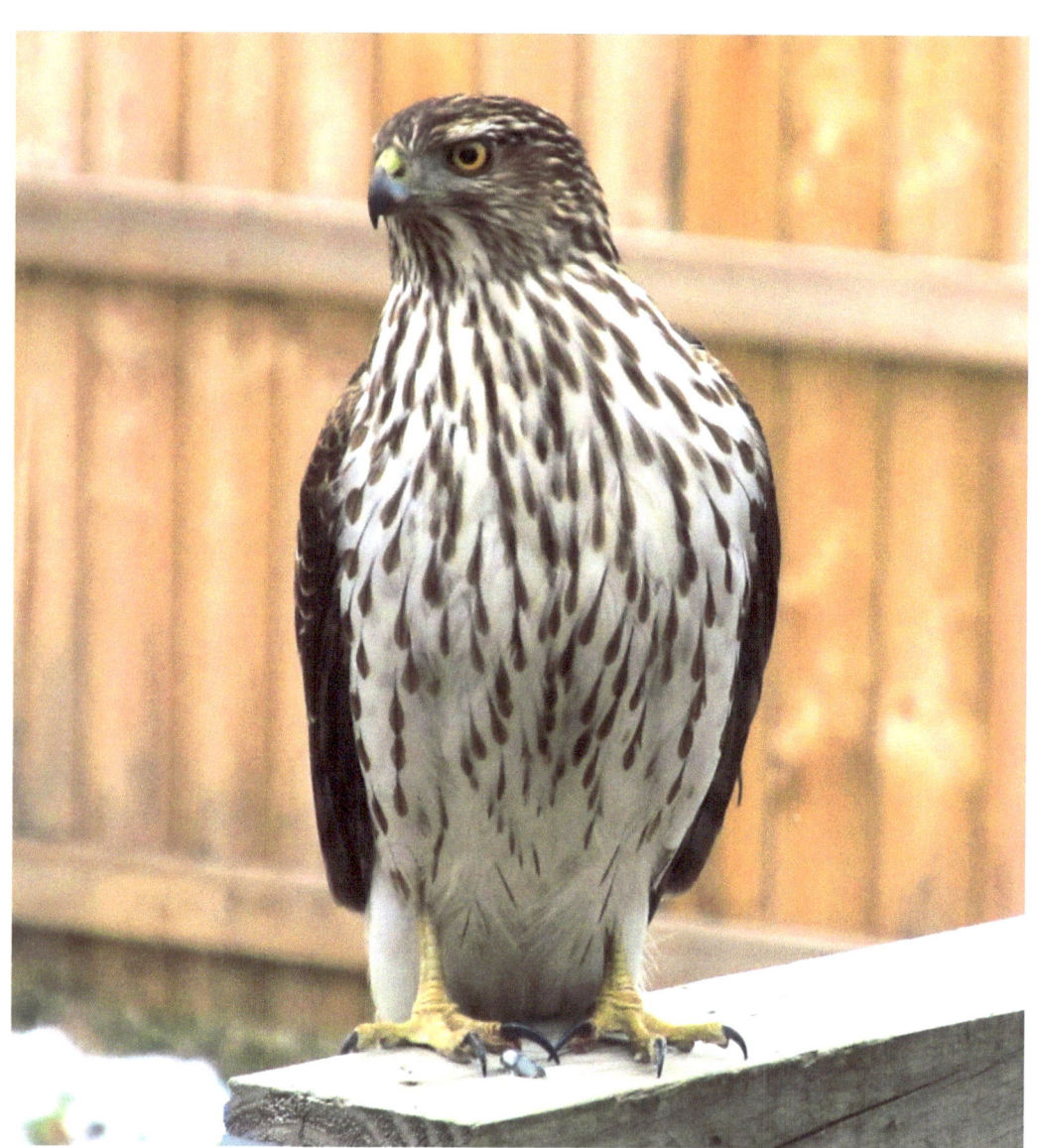

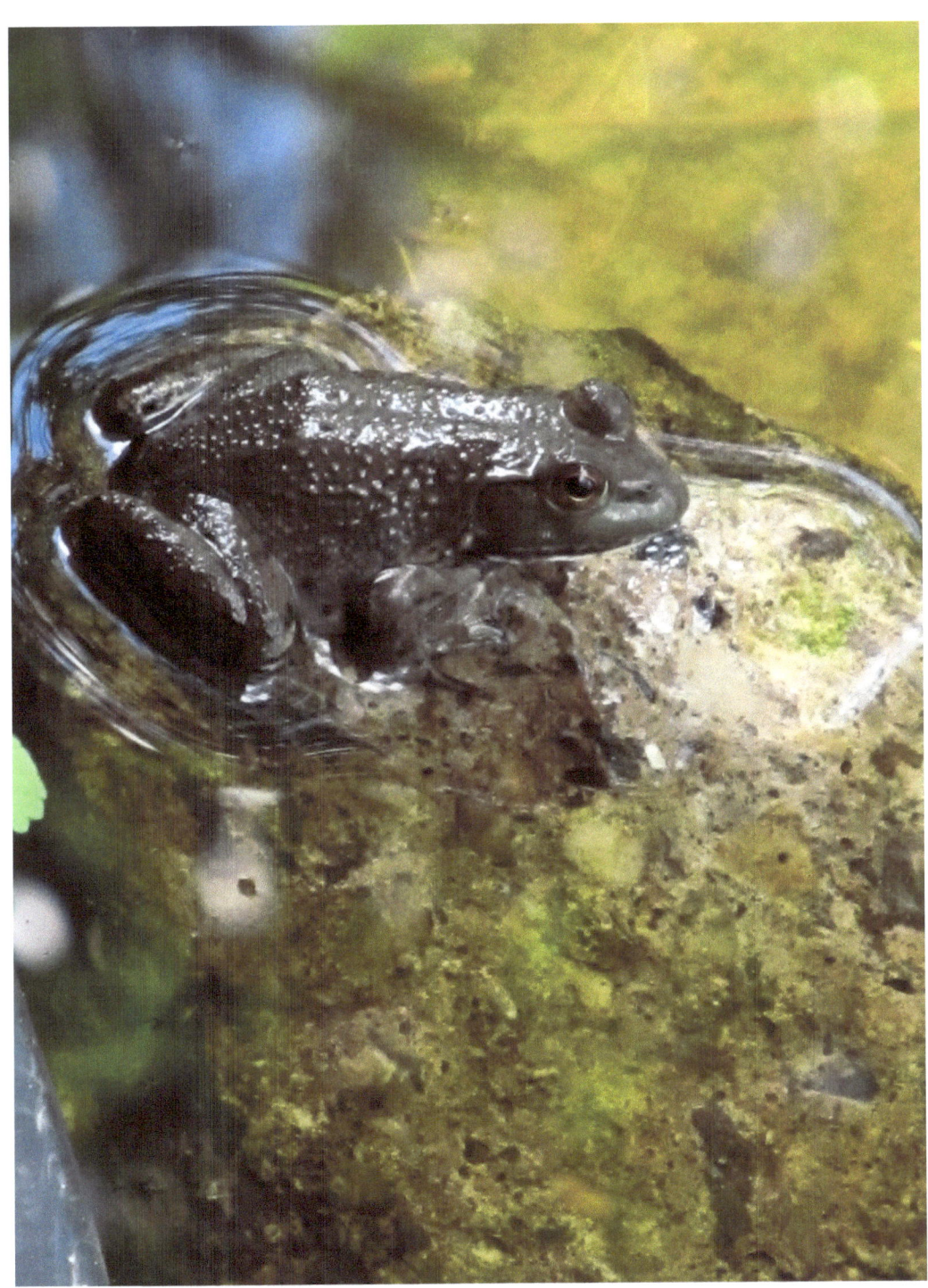

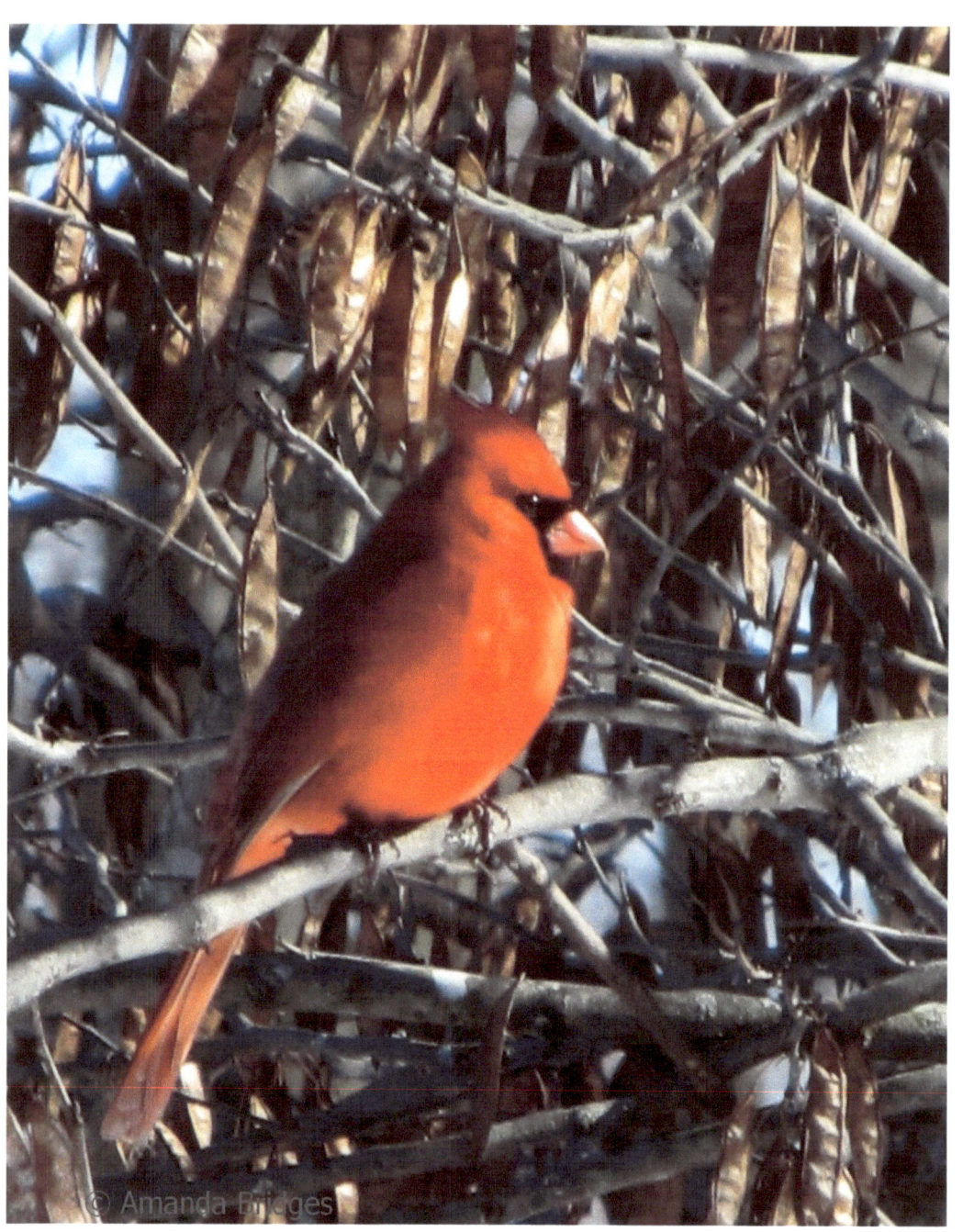

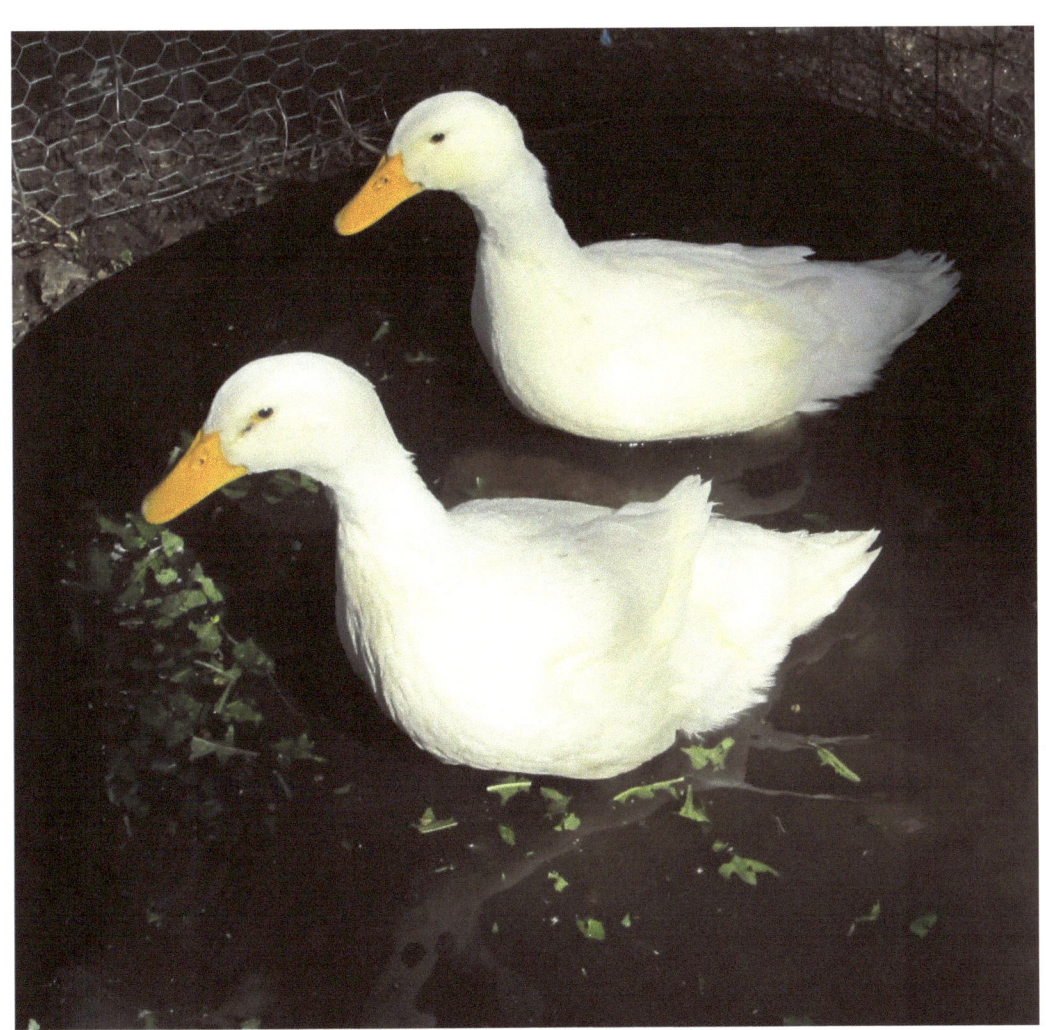

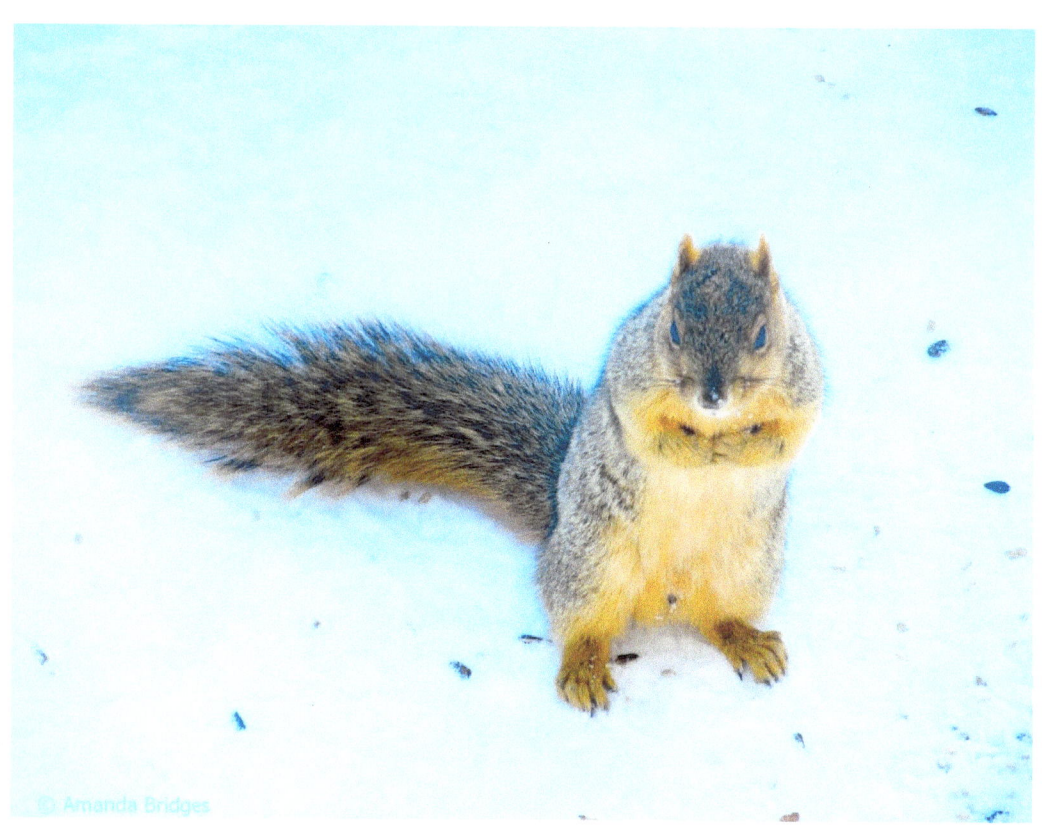

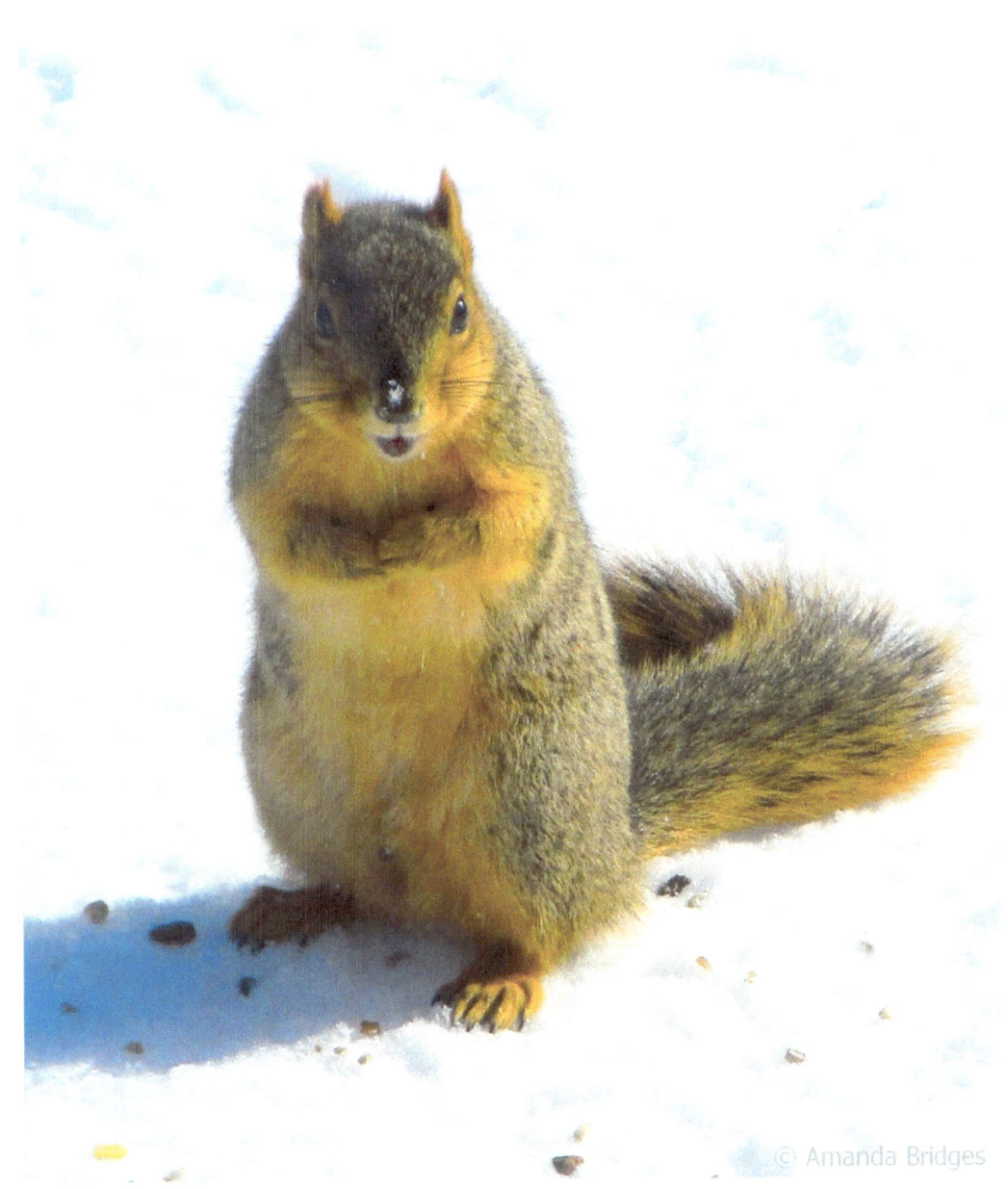

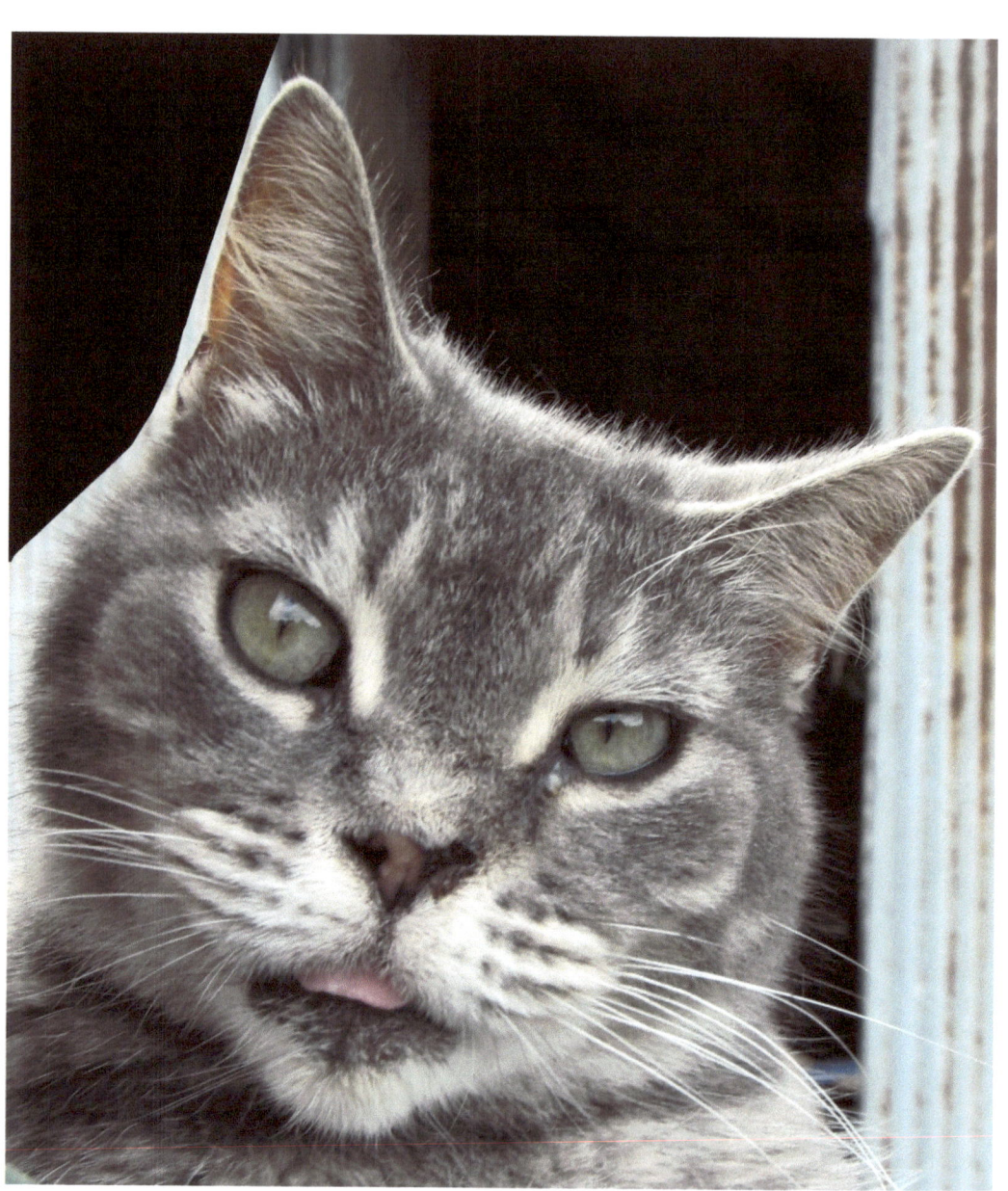

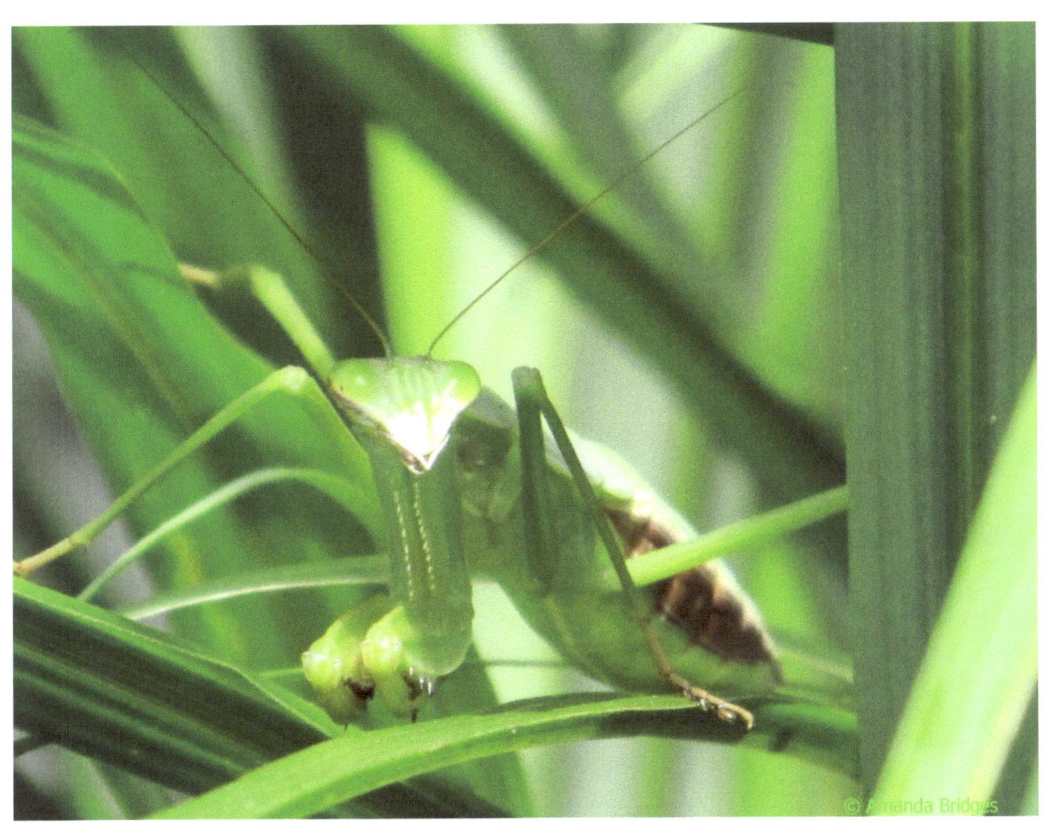

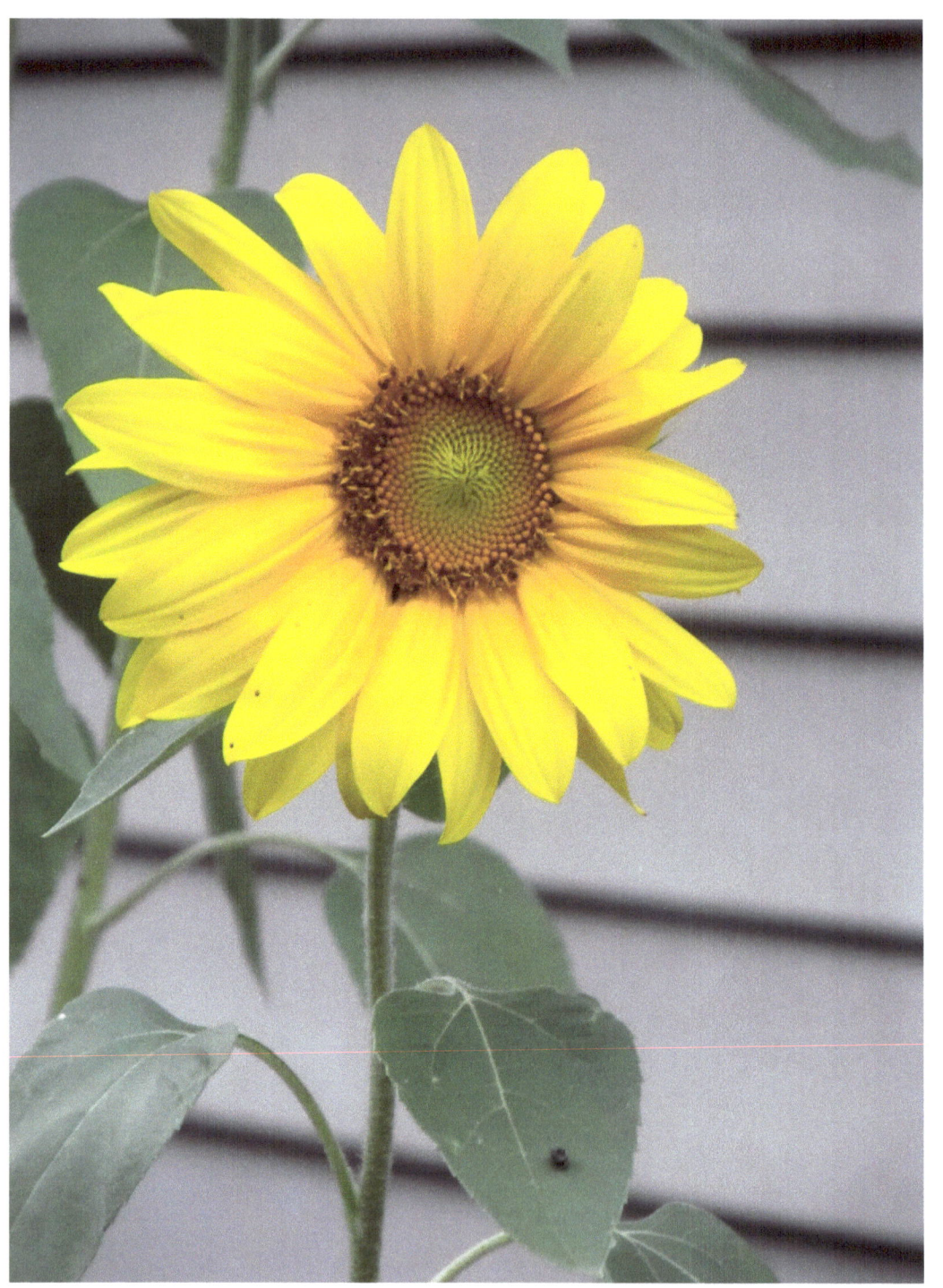

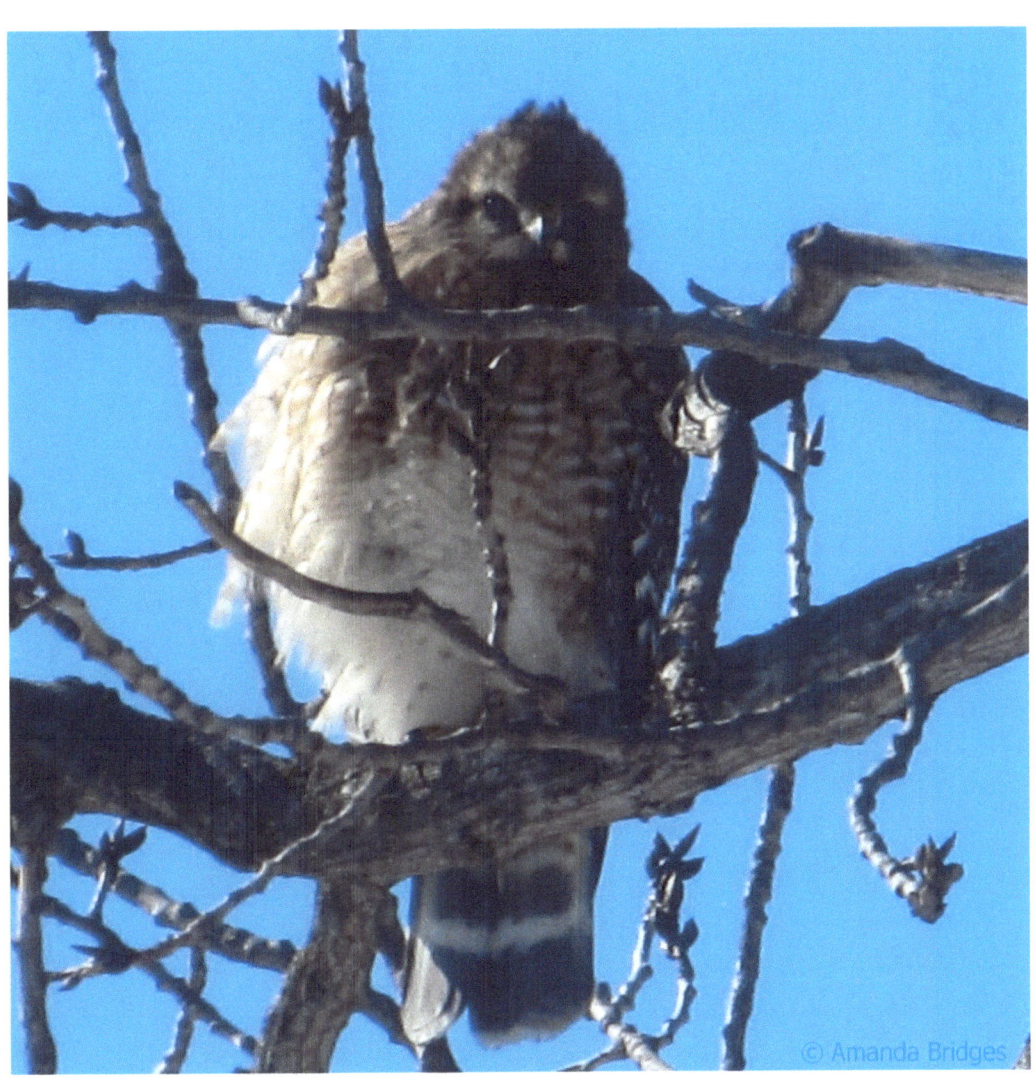

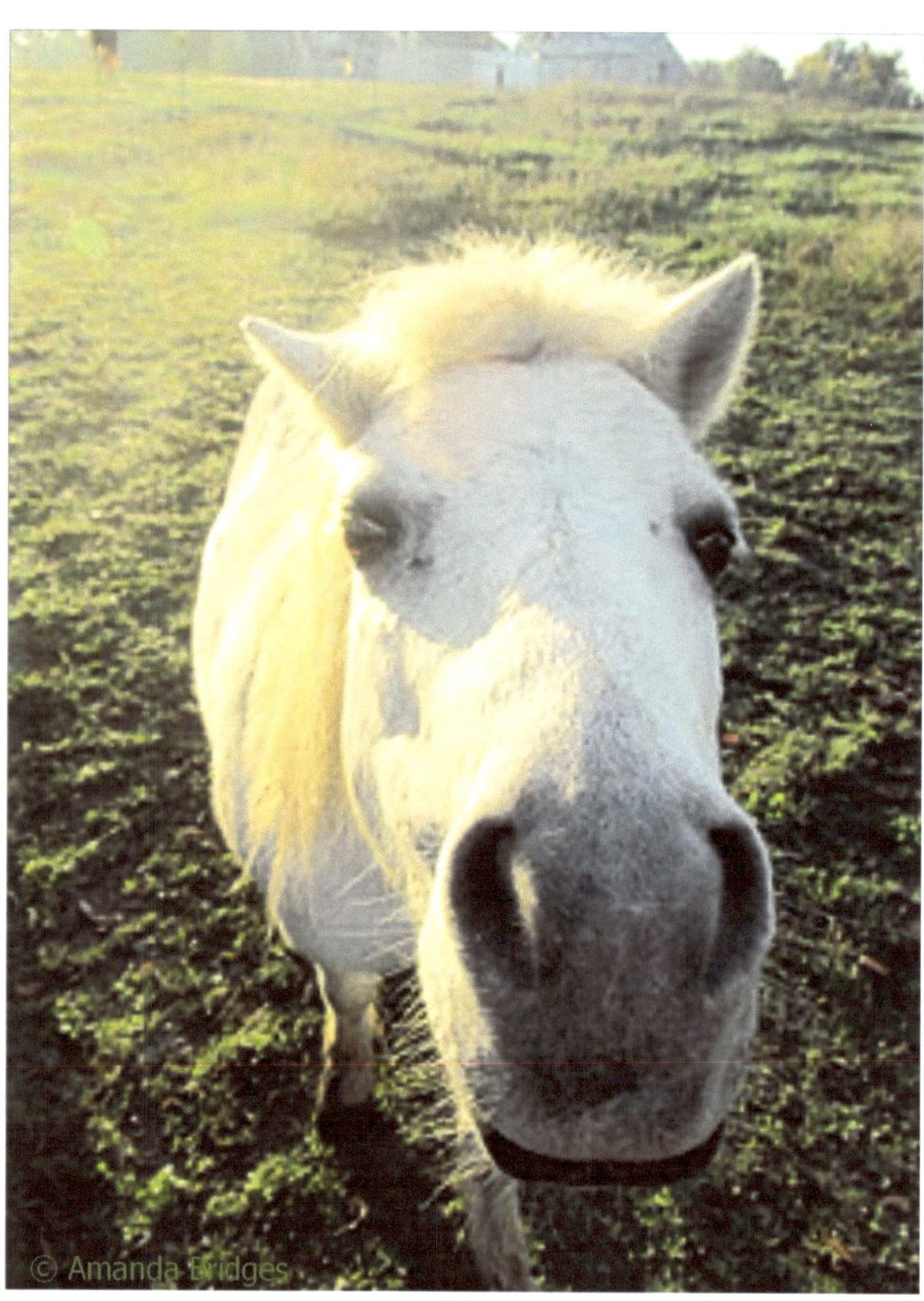

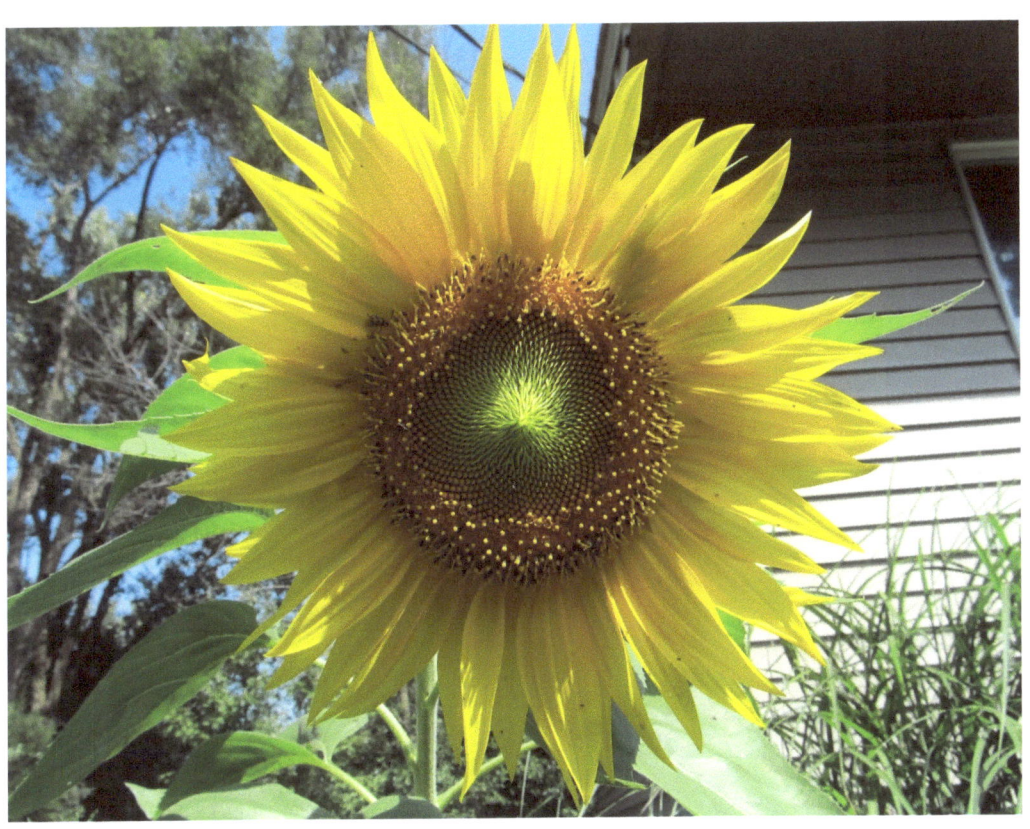

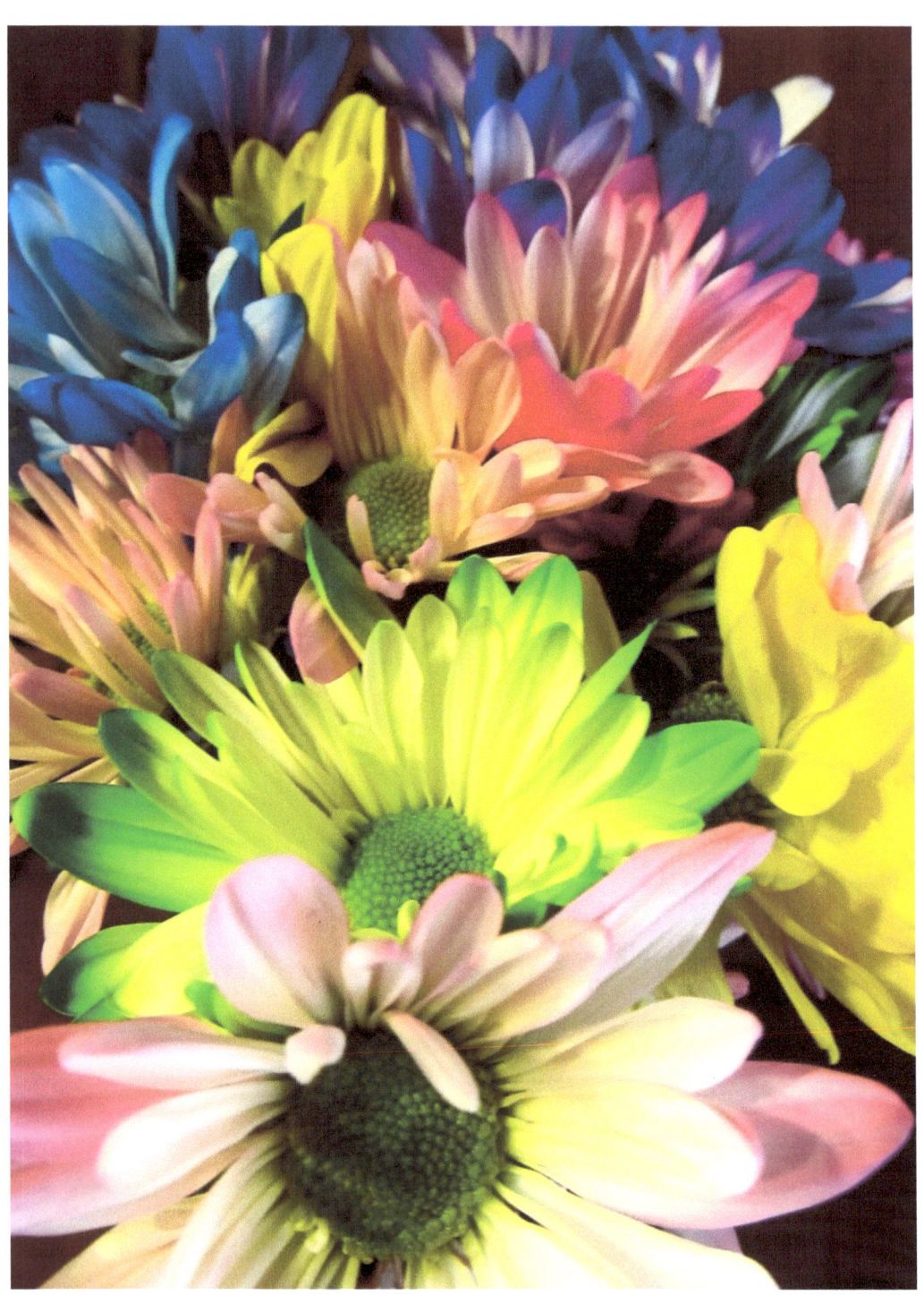

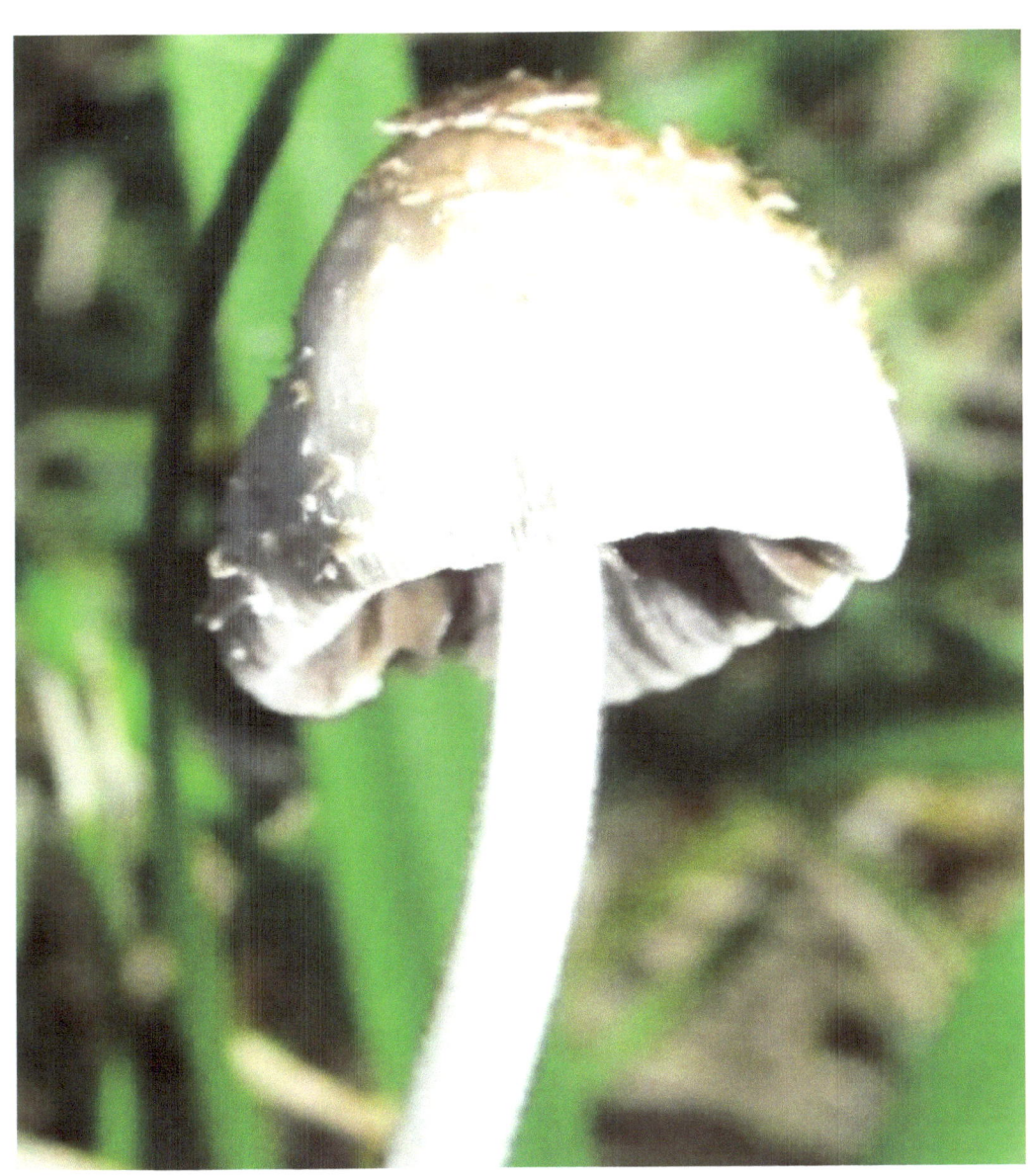

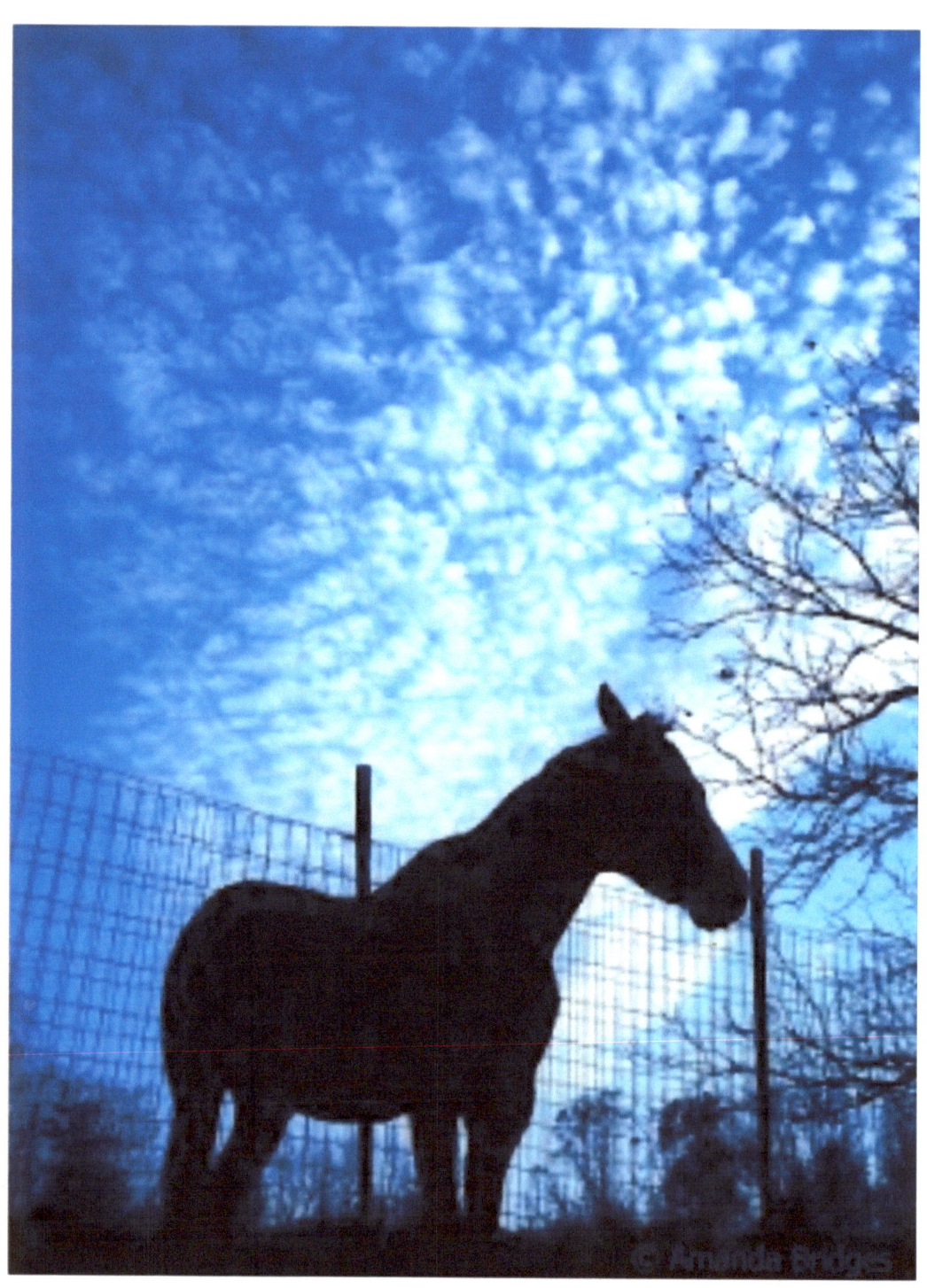

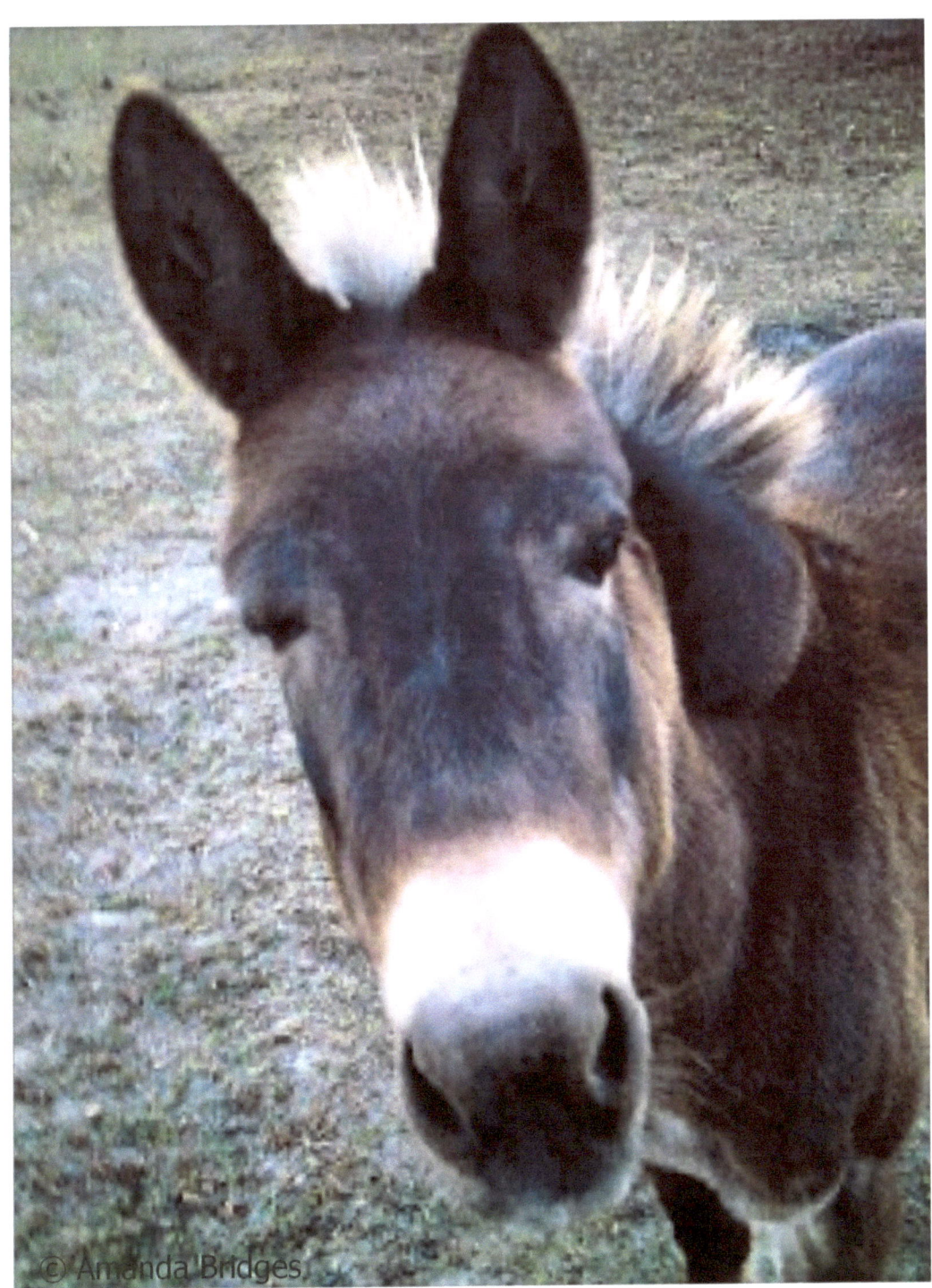

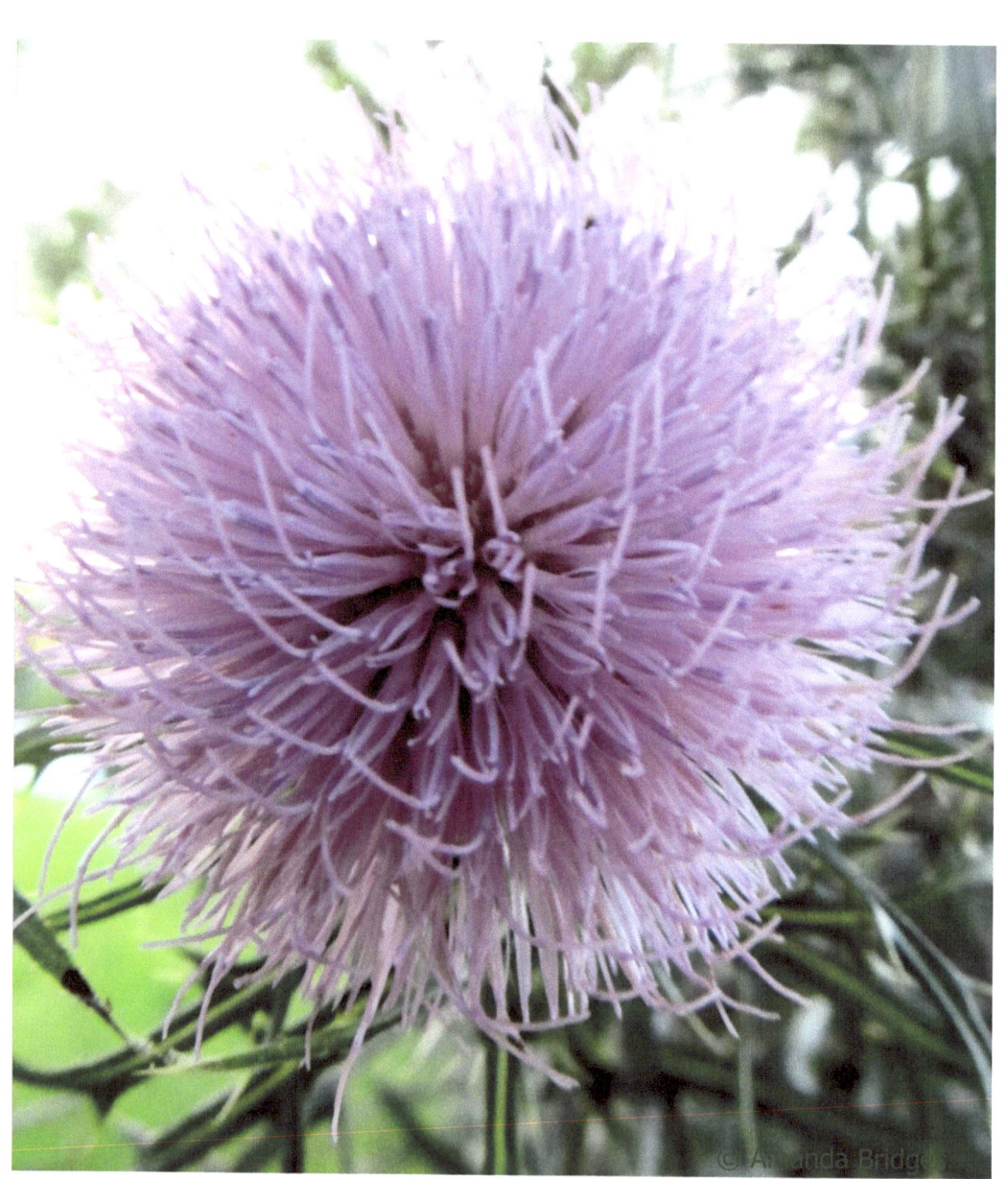

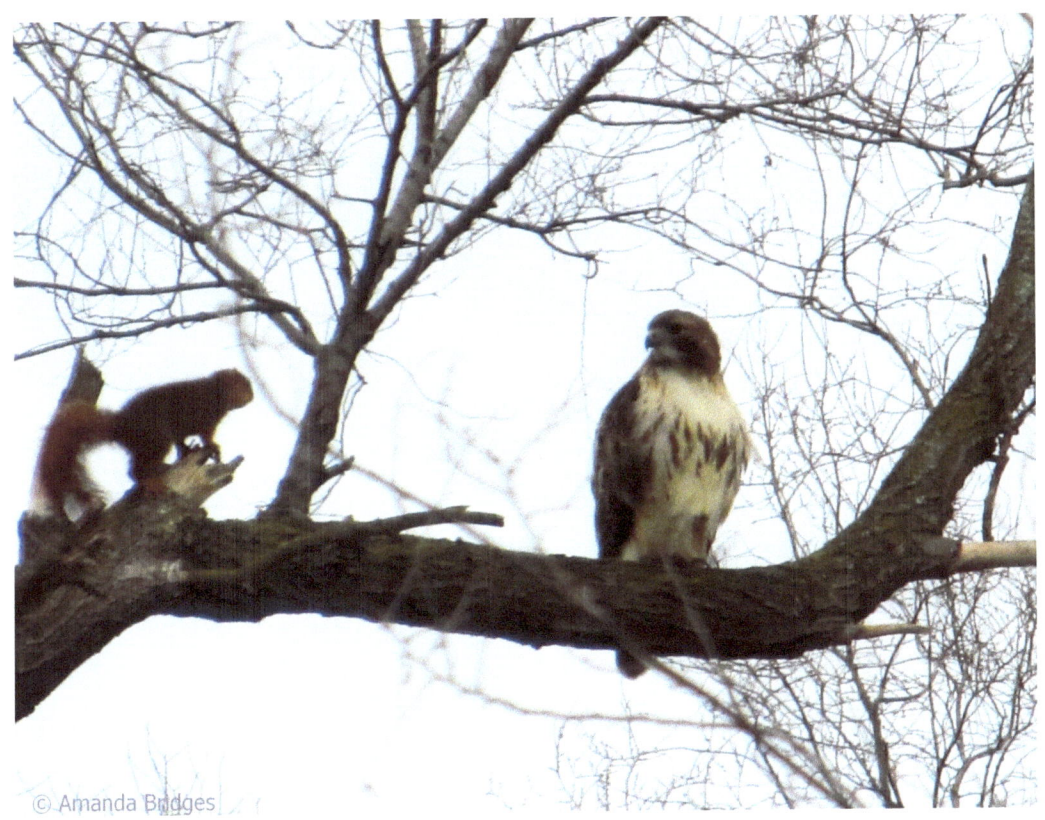
© Amanda Bridges

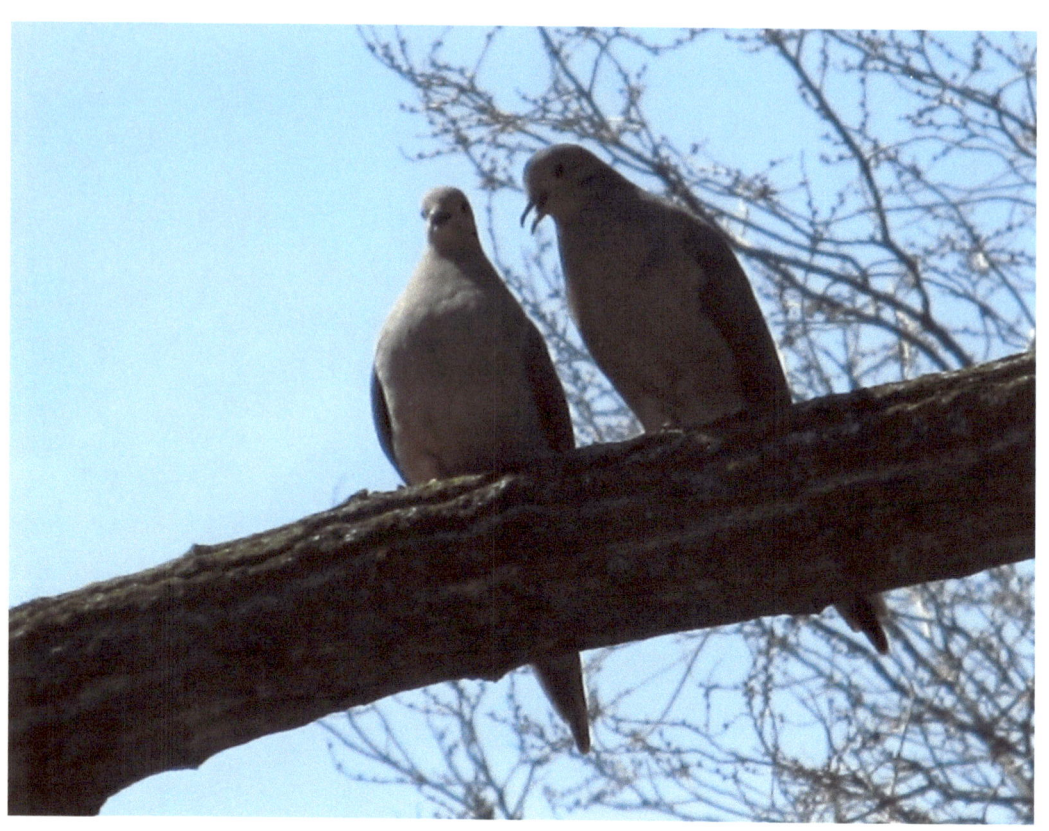

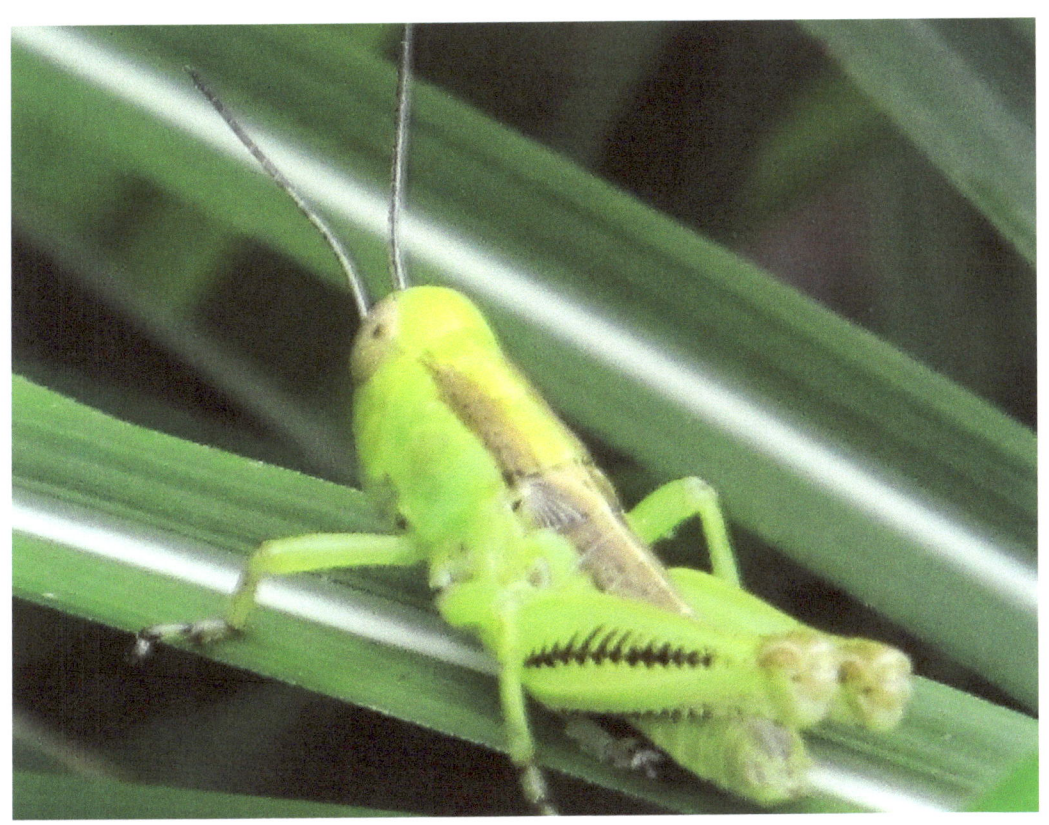

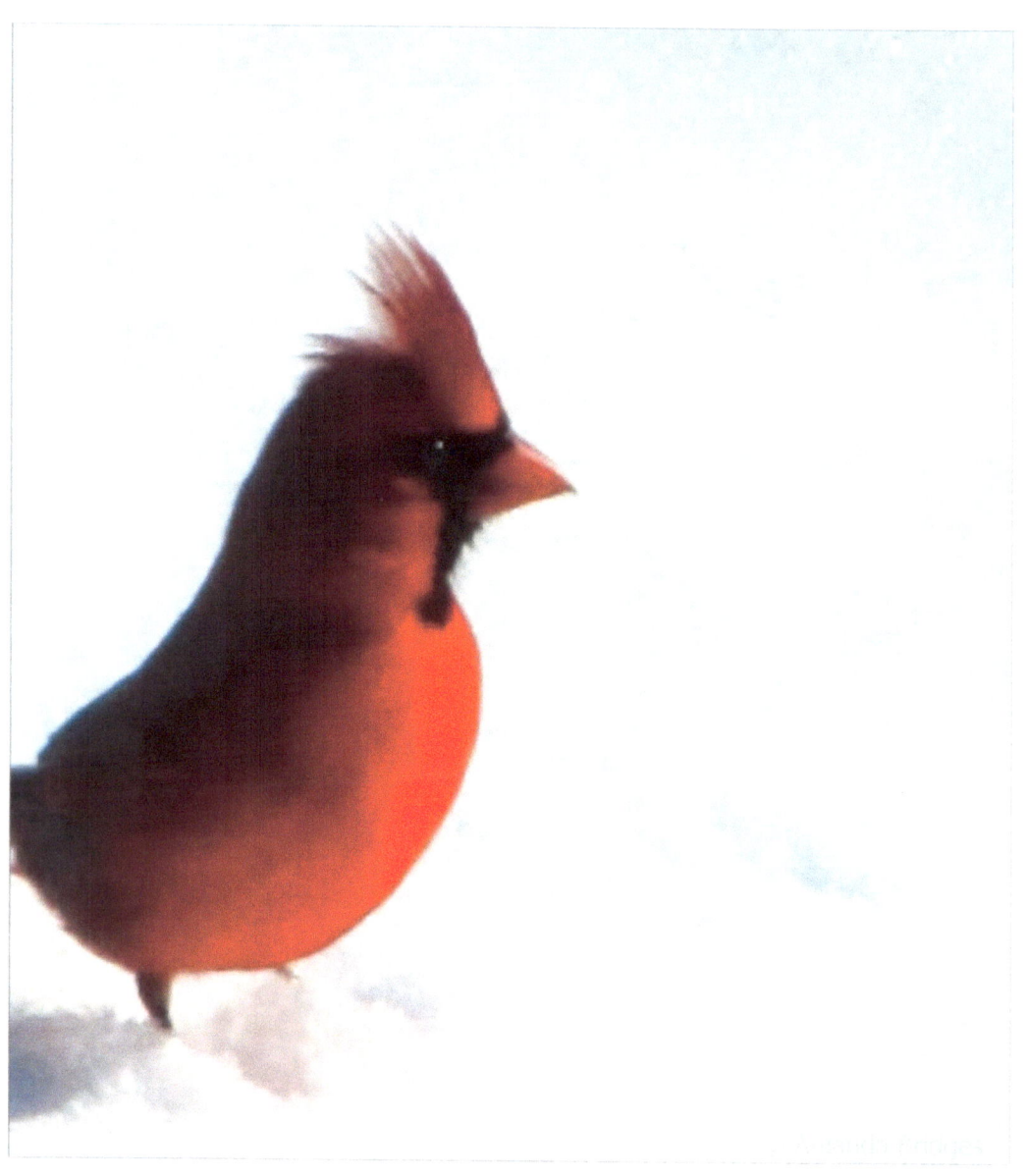

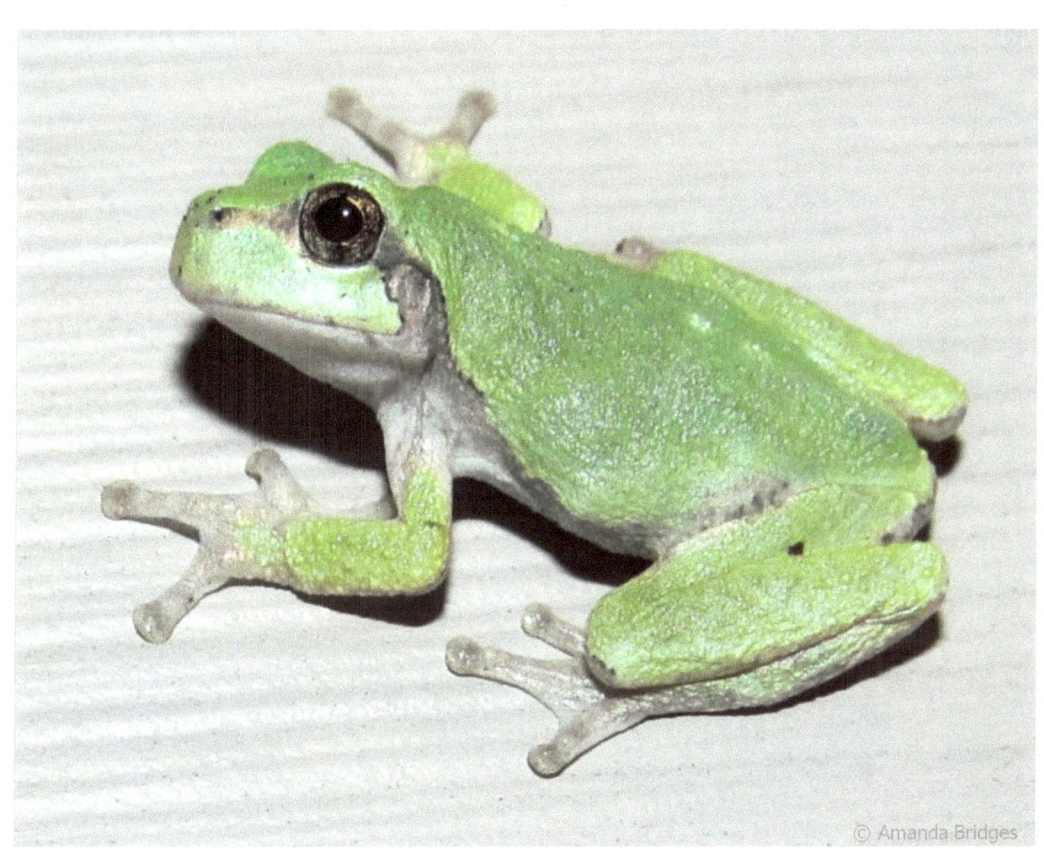

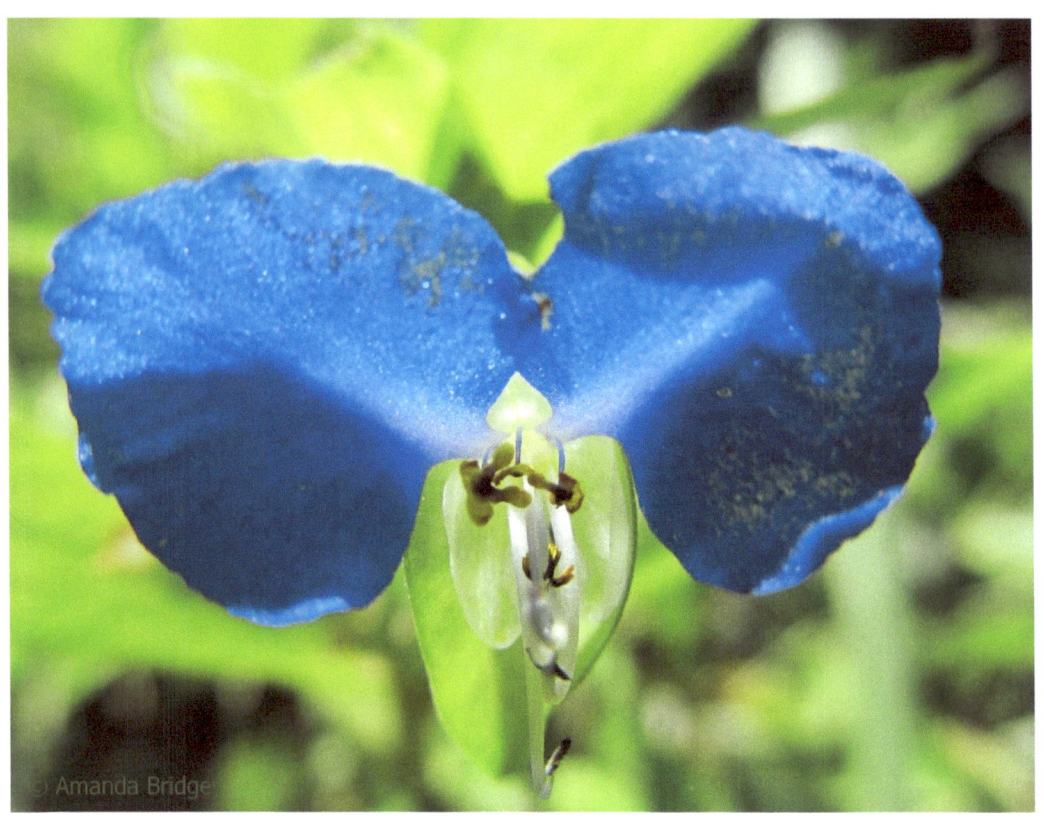

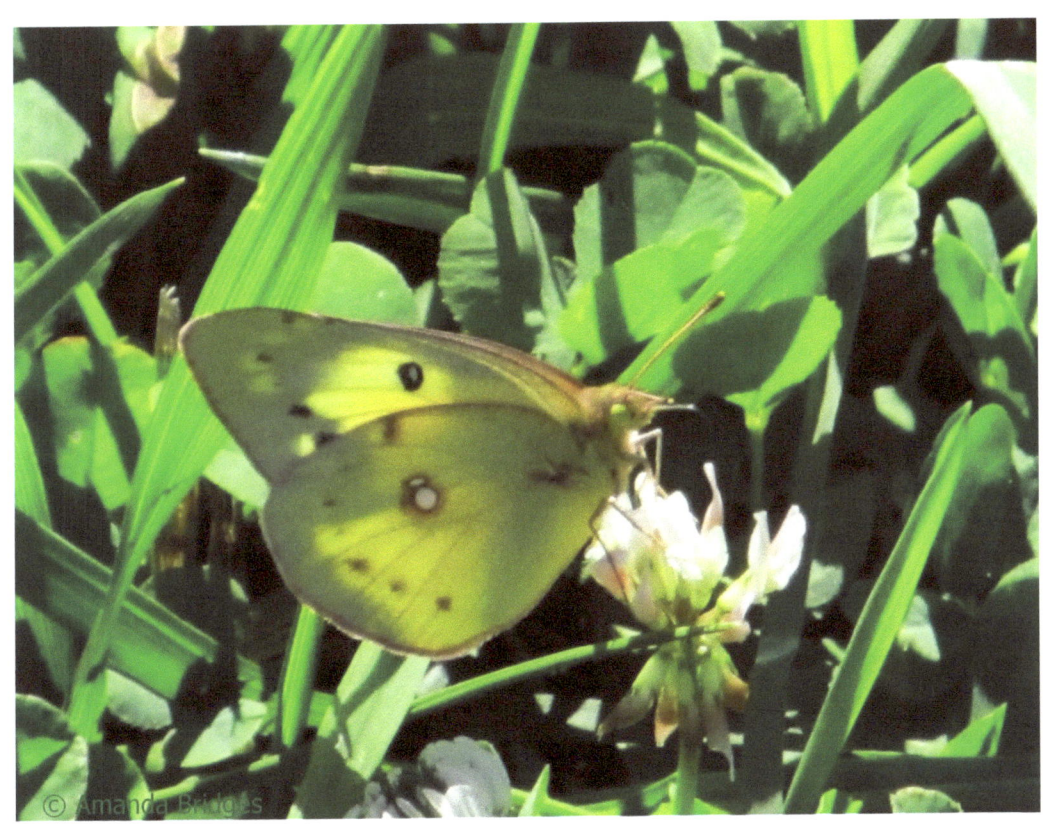

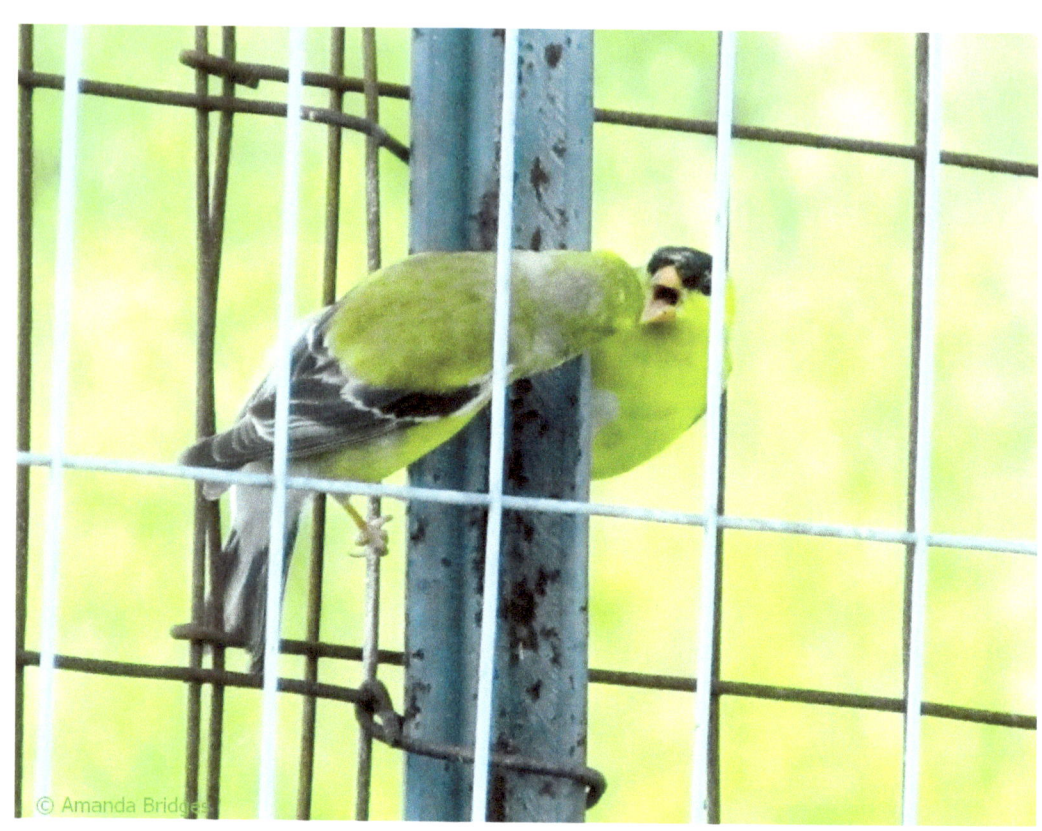

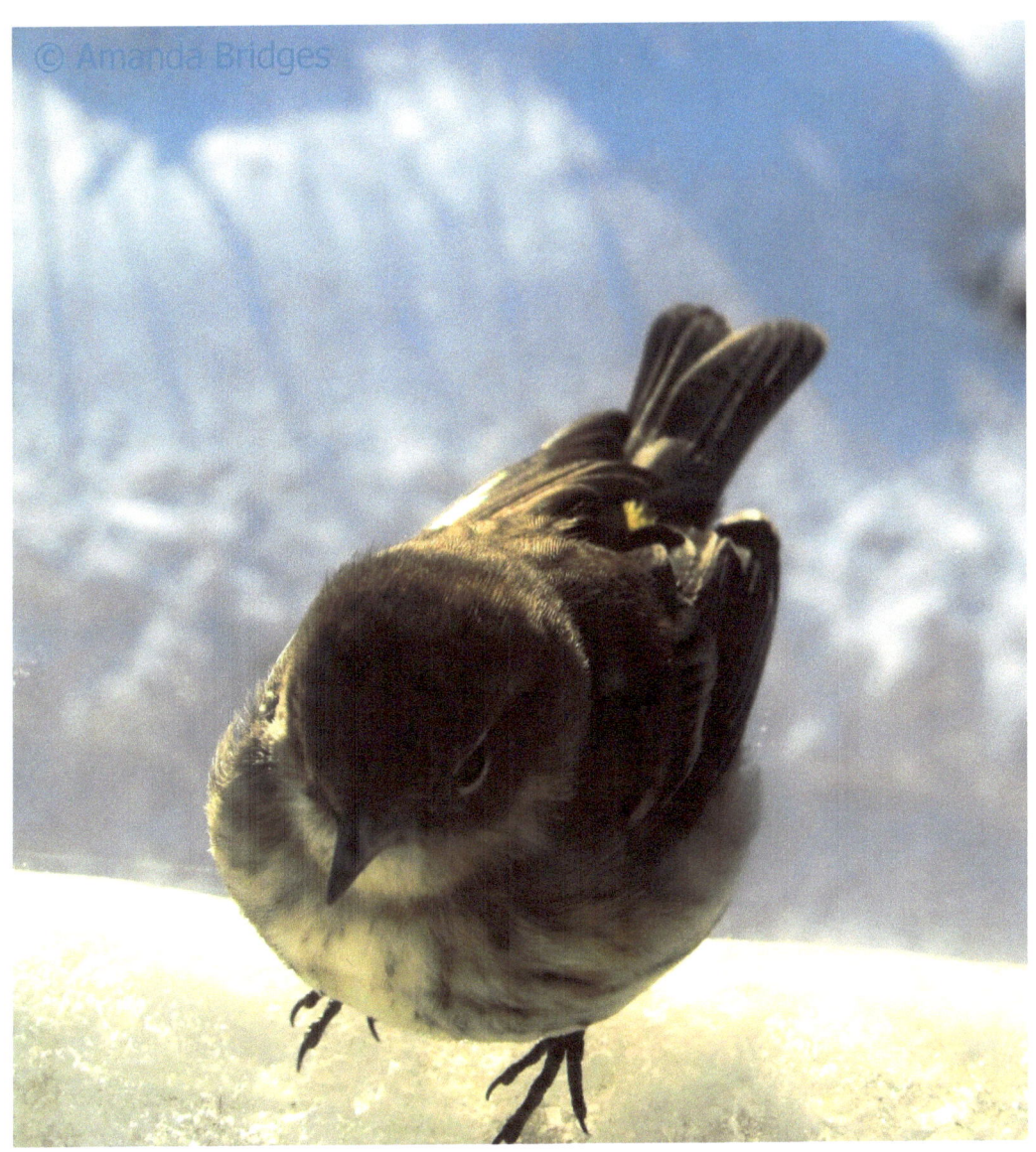

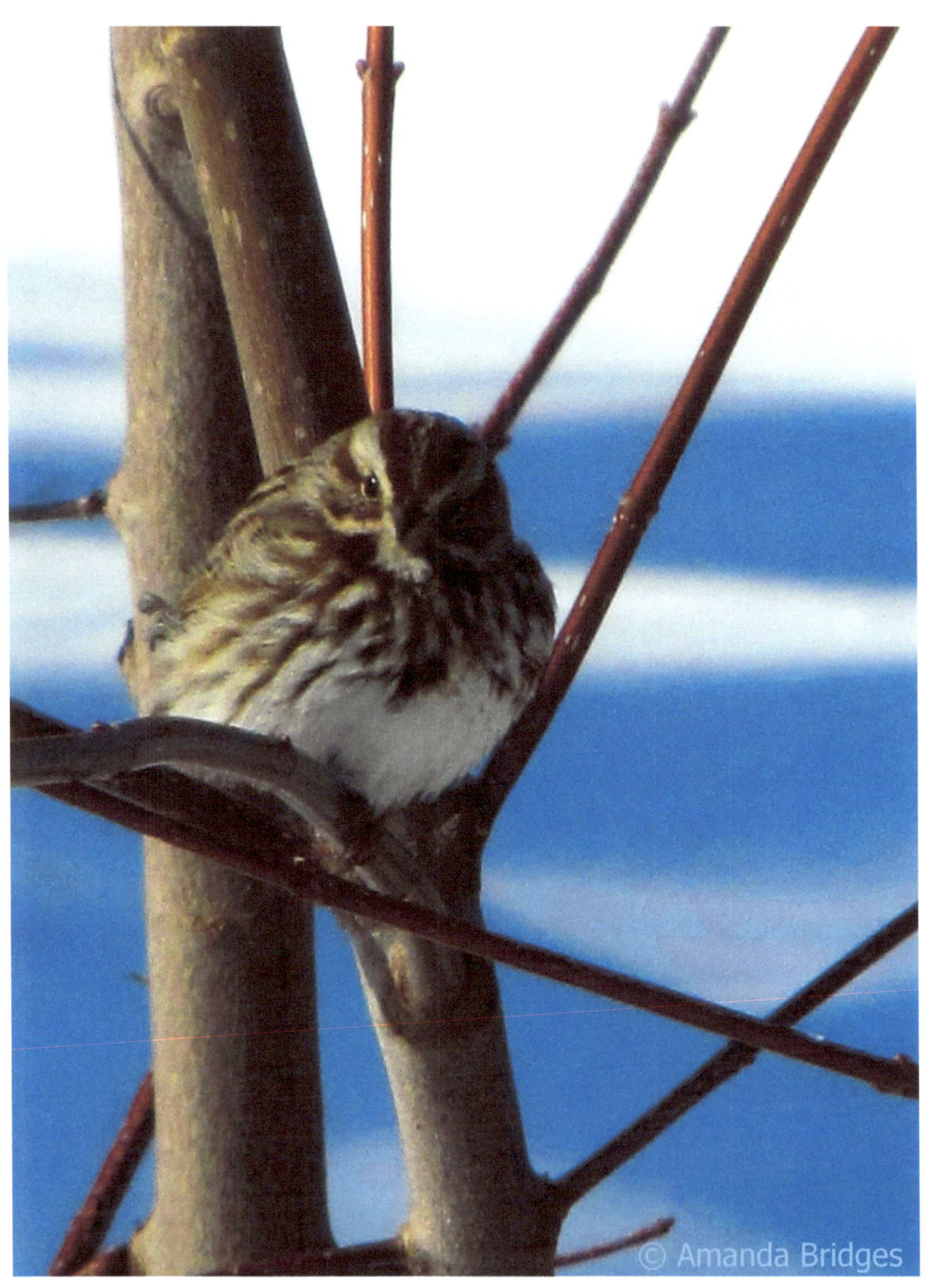

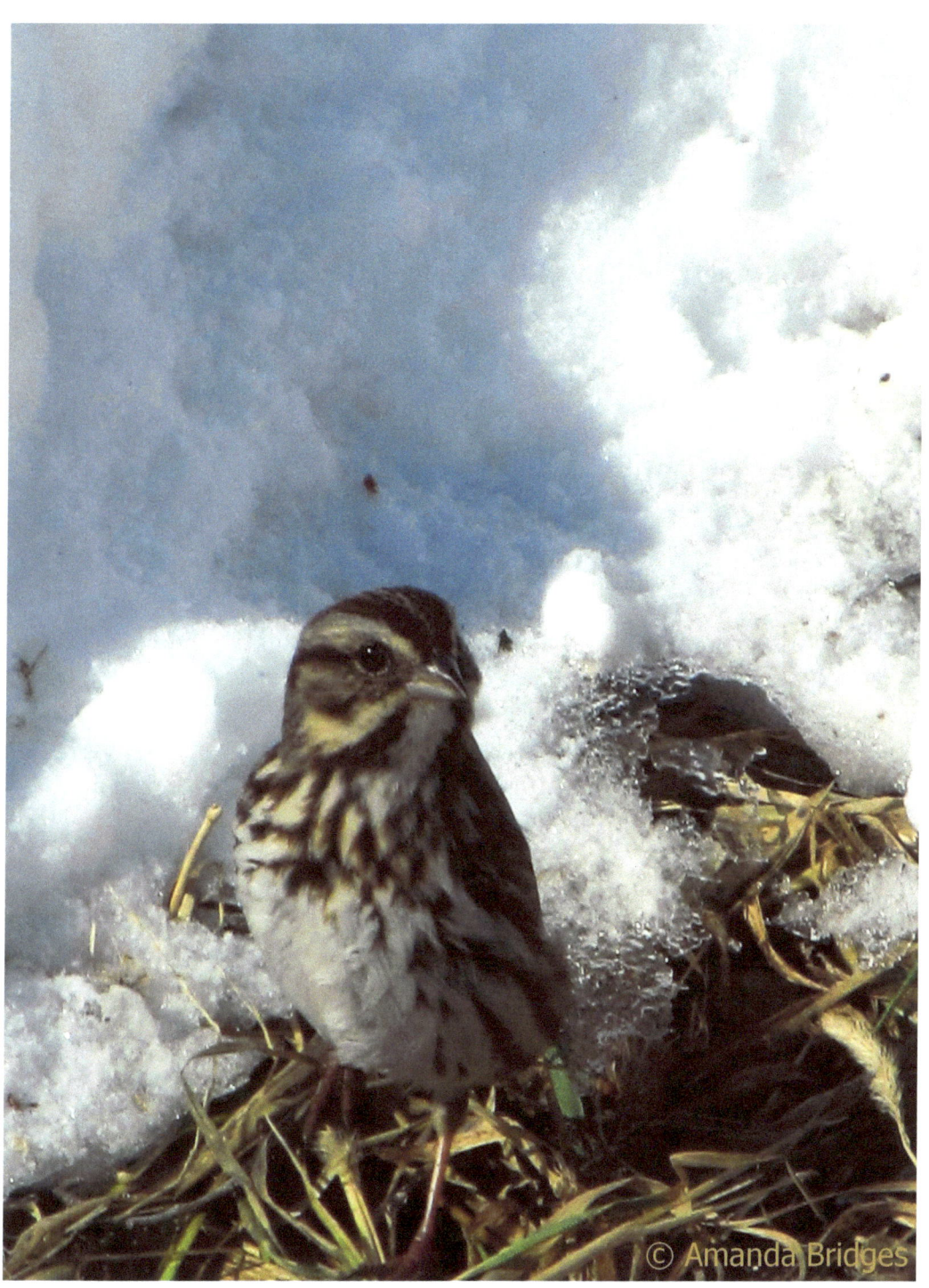

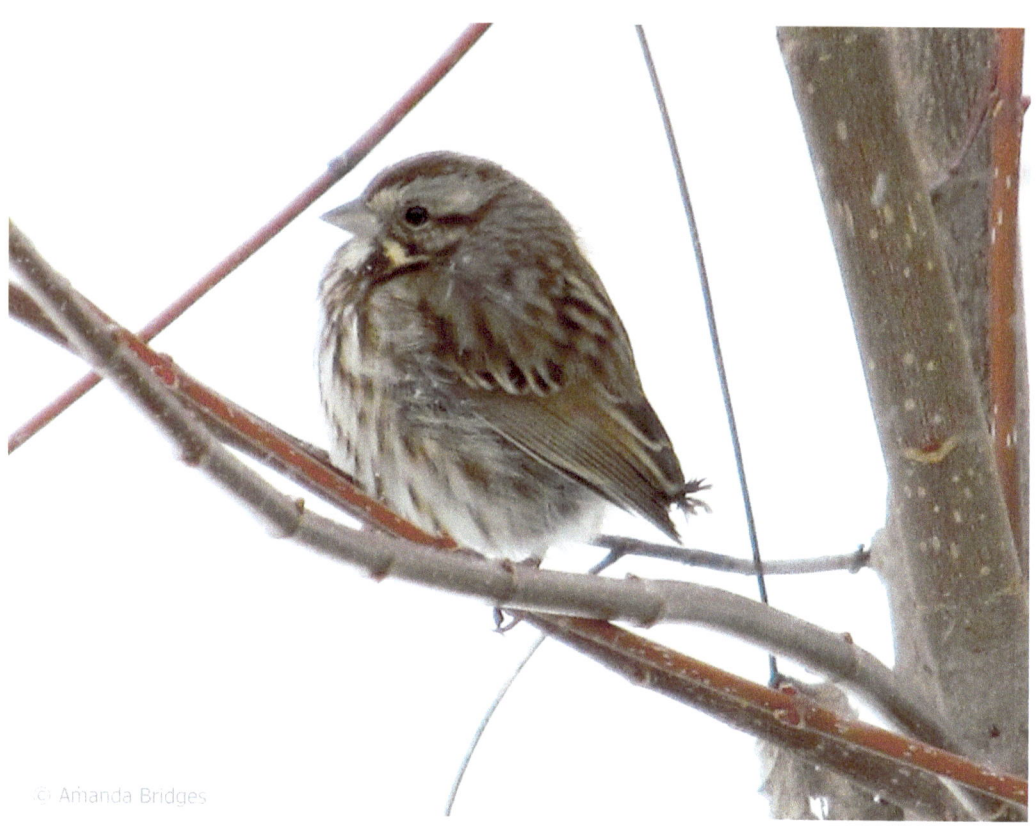

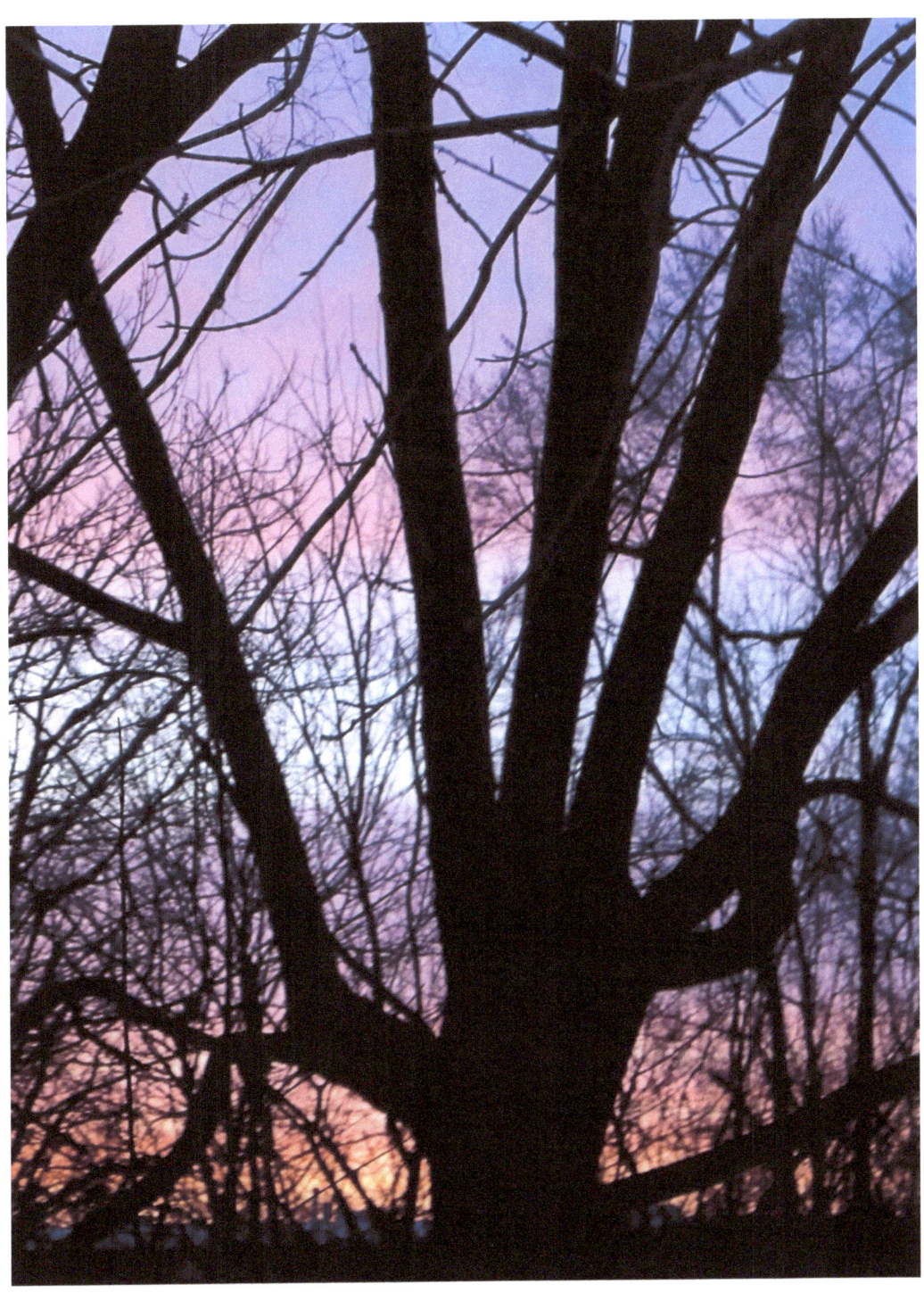

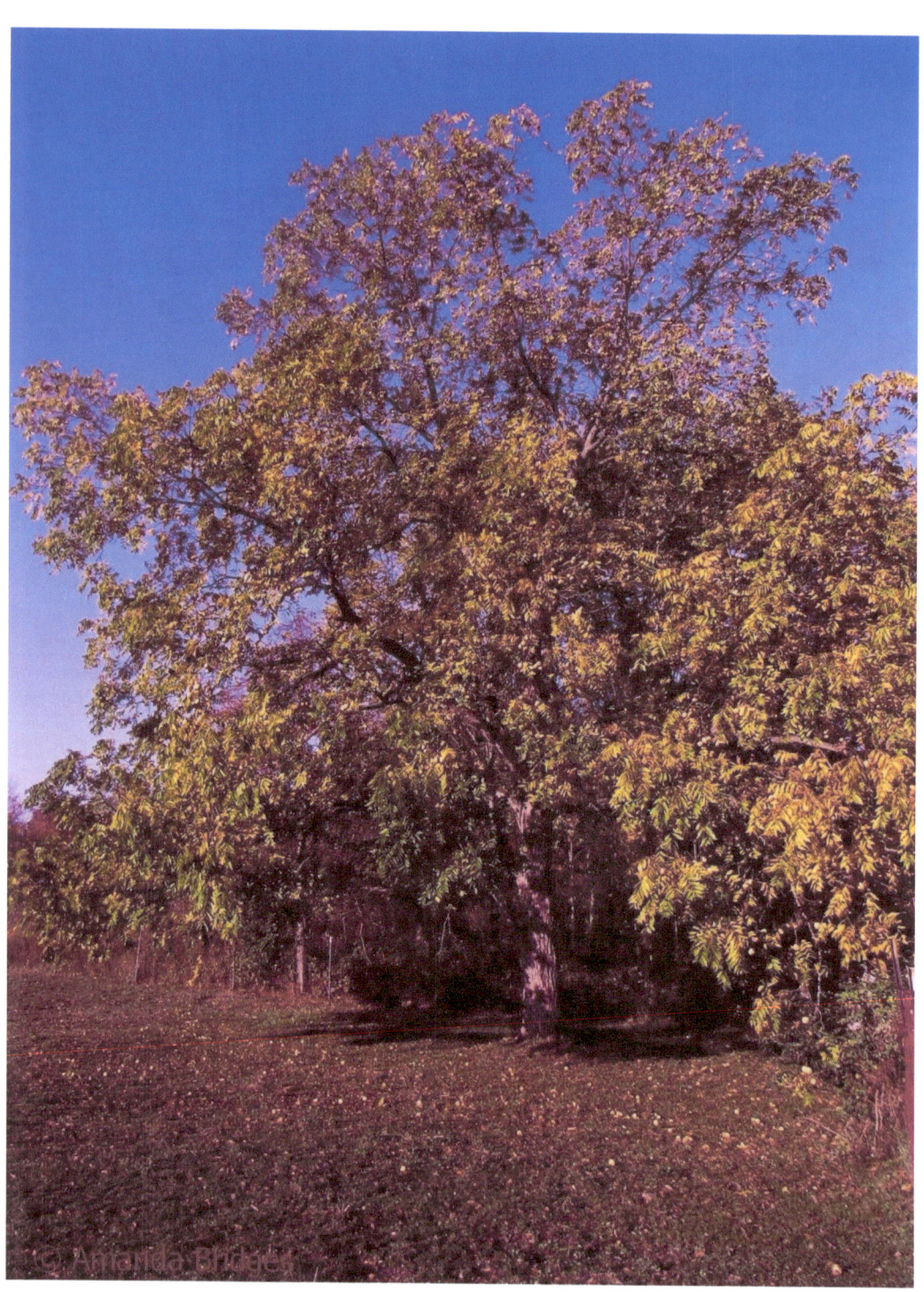

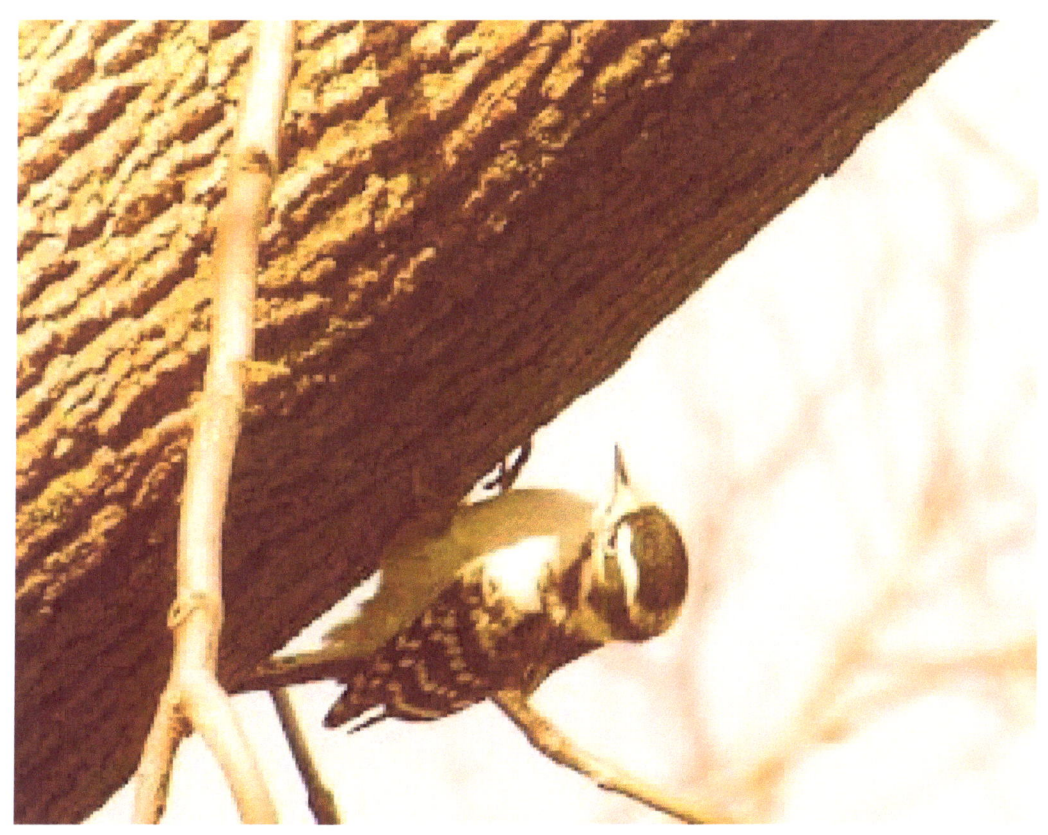

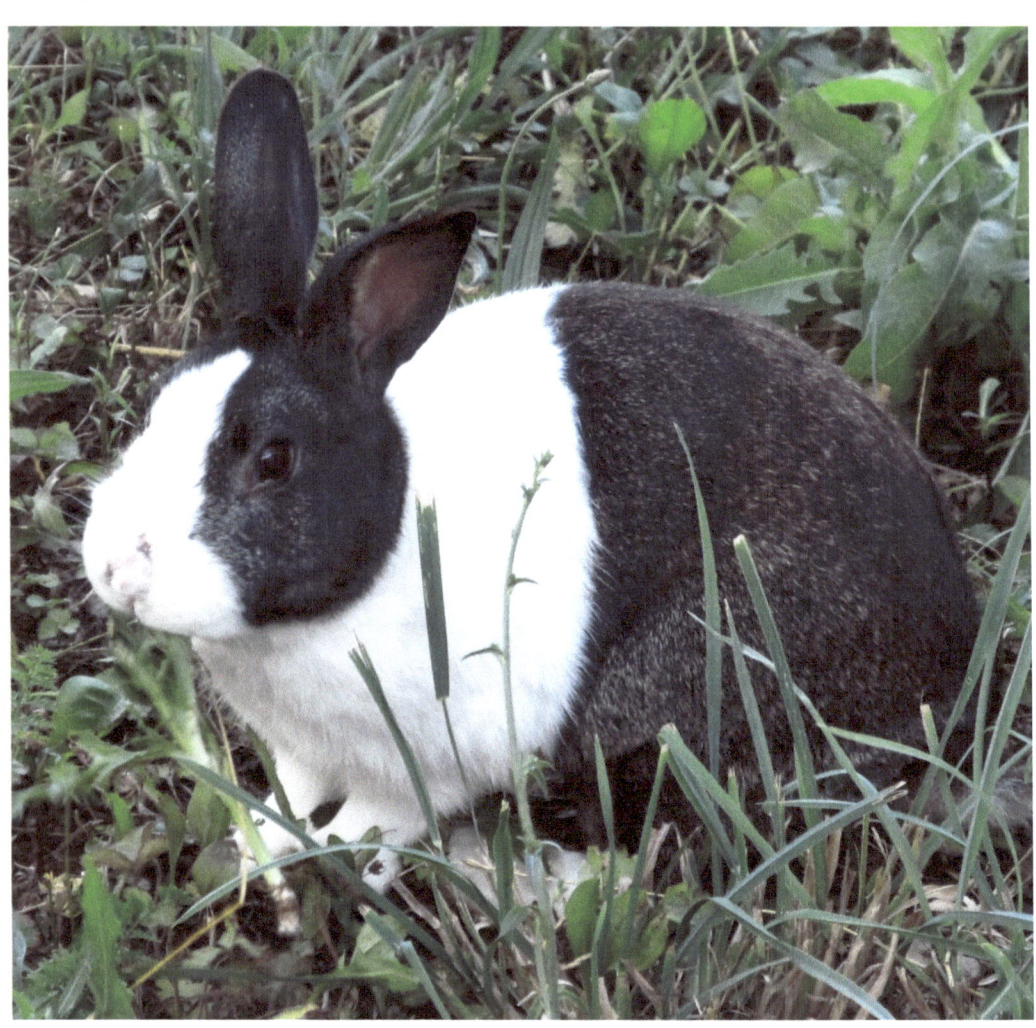

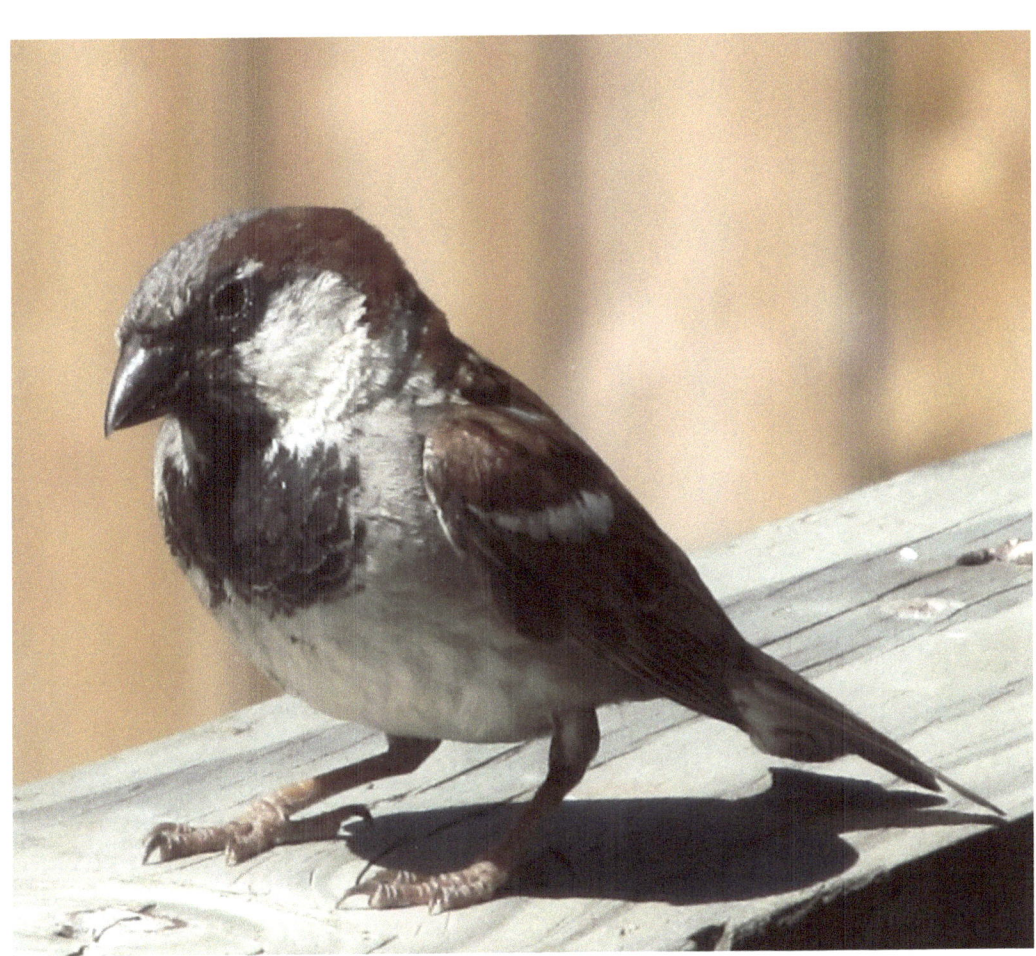

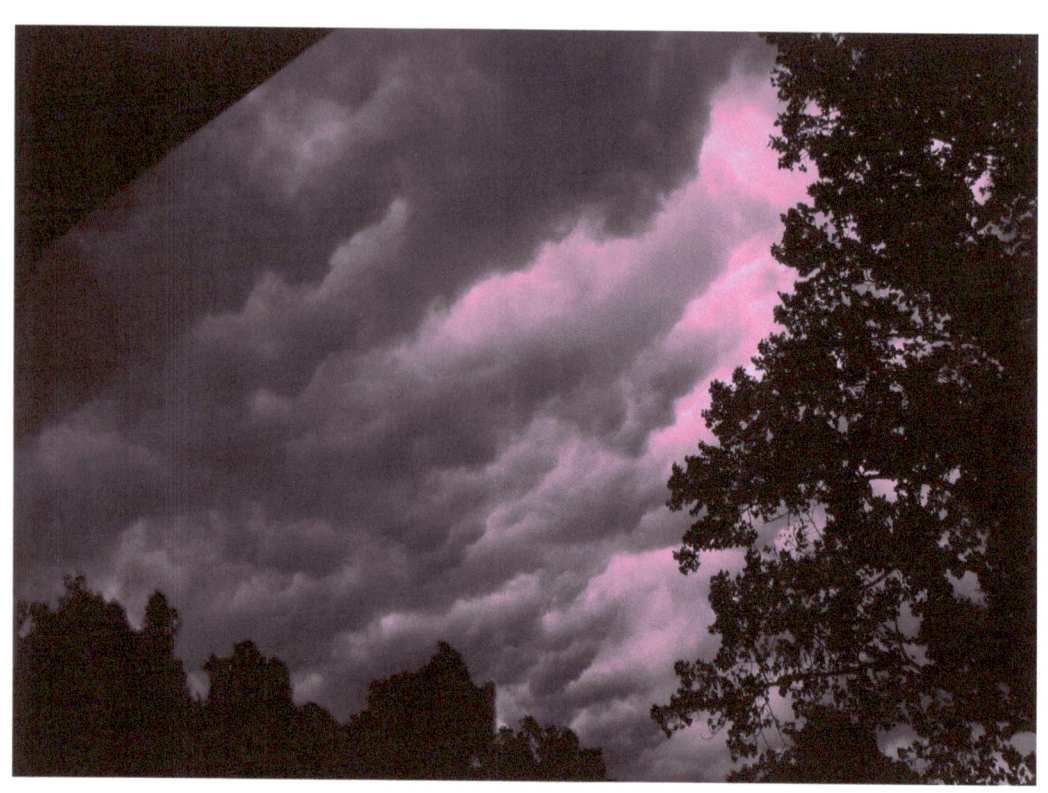

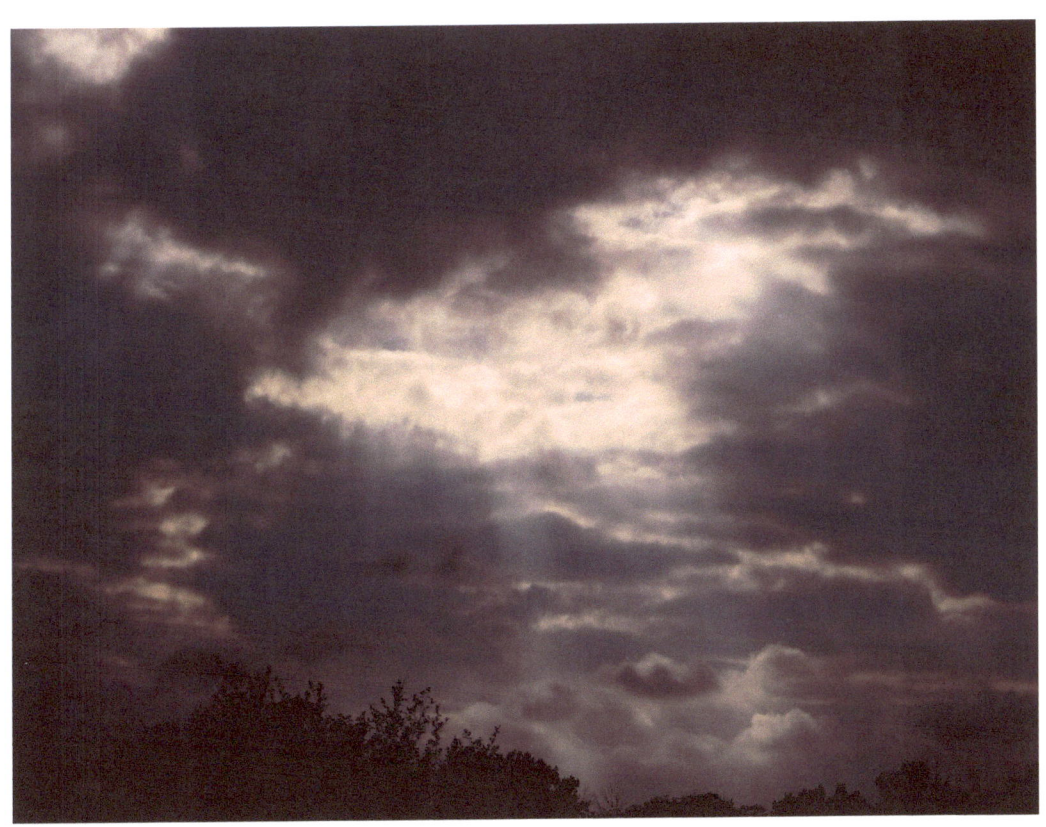

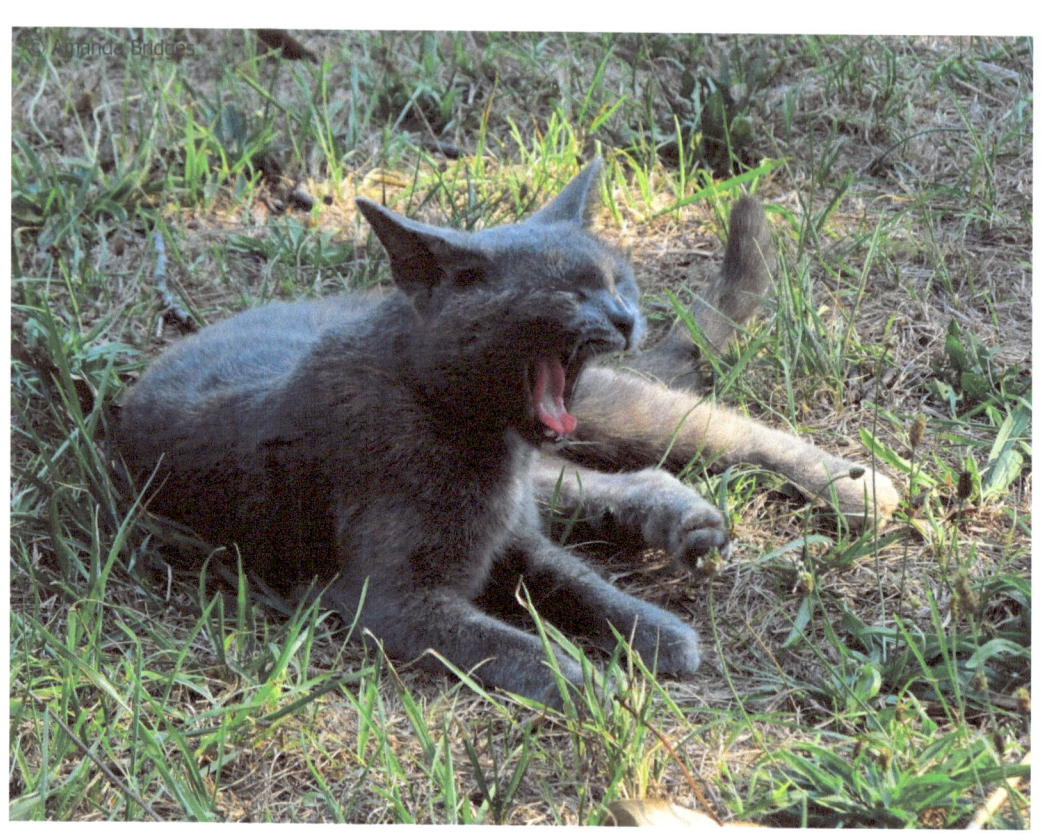

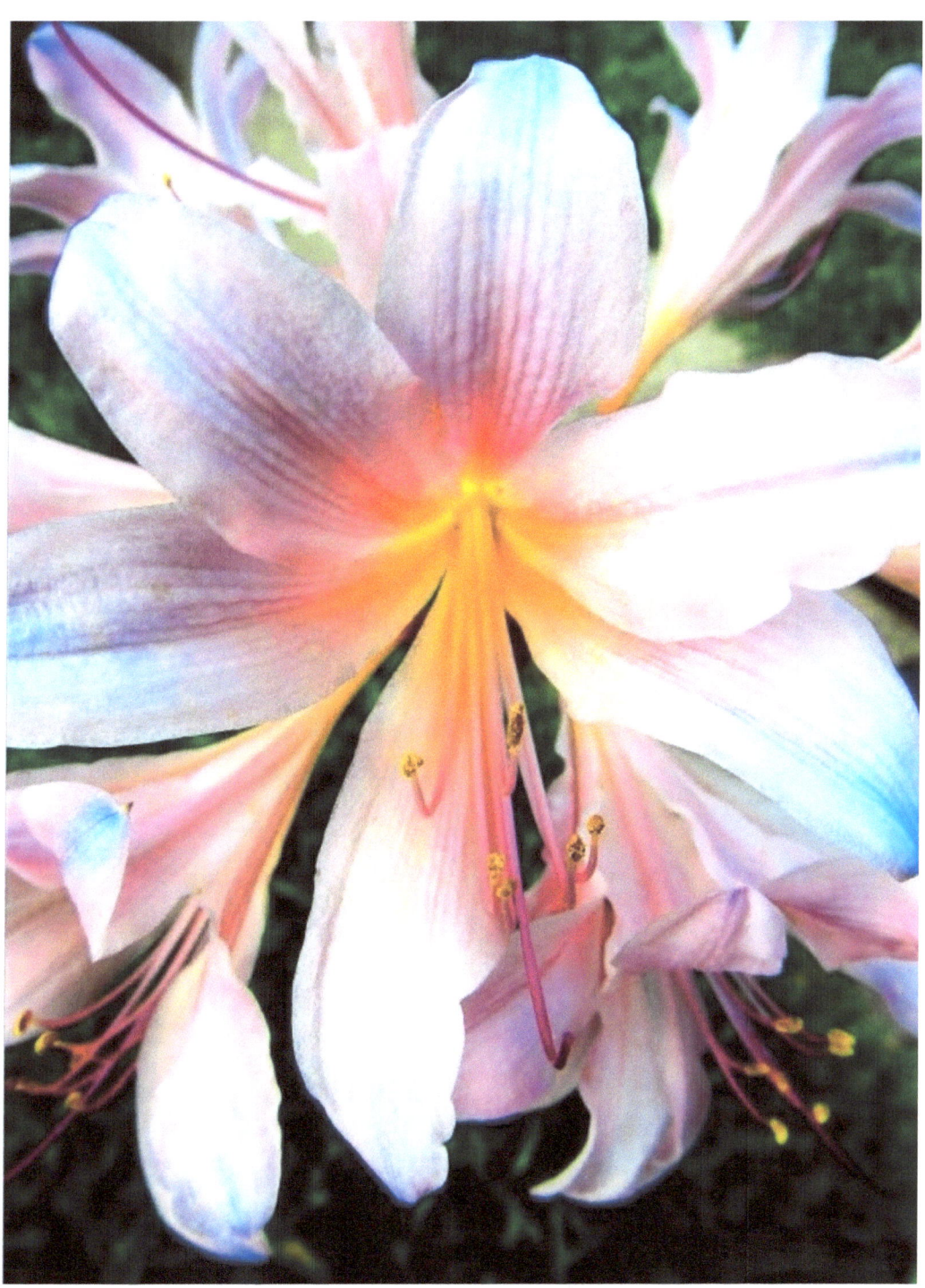

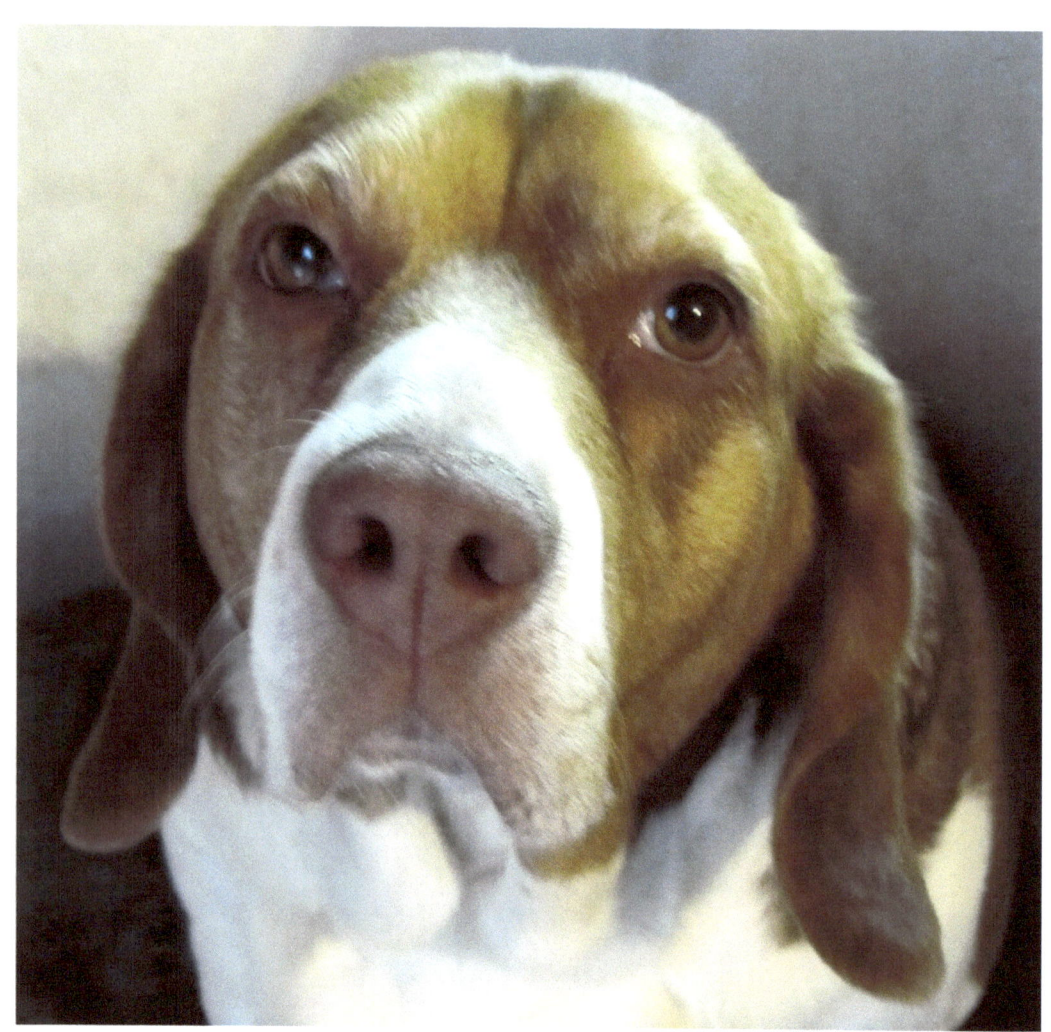

www.ingramcontent.com/pod-product-compliance
Lightning Source LLC
Chambersburg PA
CBHW051213220526
45473CB00003B/1020